# DE
## AND
# COCKTAILS
#### MY LIFE WITH THE
#### STEREOPHONICS

# DEMONS AND COCKTAILS

## MY LIFE WITH THE STEREOPHONICS

**STUART CABLE** WITH
**ANTHONY BUNKO**

WITH A FOREWORD BY HOWARD MARKS

JOHN BLAKE

Published by John Blake Publishing Ltd,
3 Bramber Court, 2 Bramber Road,
London W14 9PB, England

www.johnblakepublishing.co.uk

First published in hardback in 2009
This edition published in paperback in 2010

ISBN: 978-1-84454-942-9

British Library Cataloguing-in-Publication Data:

A catalogue record for this book is available from the British Library.

Design by www.envydesign.co.uk

Printed in Great Britain by CPI Bookmarque, Croydon, CR0 4TD

1 3 5 7 9 10 8 6 4 2

Papers used by John Blake Publishing are natural, recyclable products made
from wood grown in sustainable forests. The manufacturing processes conform
to the environmental regulations of the country of origin.

Every attempt has been made to contact the relevant copyright-holders,
but some were unobtainable. We would be grateful if the appropriate
people could contact us.

Dedicated to my late father:

Arthur Cable, 1931–1980

*We could have had a ball together.*

# CONTENTS

# ACKNOWLEDGEMENTS

I would like to thank everyone who has been there with me through all of this madness – through the good times and, more importantly, the bad. I will never forget you.

Special thanks must go out to all the people who gave up their time to give a quote for the book, plus the great Howard Marks for the foreword – and of course Anthony Bunko, who convinced me one drunken night that all the stories in my head should be put down on paper. Although we spent most of our time together arguing about AC/DC and The Clash, I think he helped me do a decent job of making it all come alive once again. Thanks.

Stuart Cable
February 2009

# FOREWORD
## BY HOWARD MARKS, AUTHOR
## AND RETIRED DRUG LORD

'Come on, 'Ow, take that bloody spliff out of your gob and answer the door, for fuck's sake!'

The voice was loud. Overtones of differing Valleys accents resonated deafeningly, vitalising the sleepy tranquillity of the street where I was born. The curtains of the houses across the road parted in concert. The neighbours had seen it all before – gangsters, spies, cops, Rastafarians and men from Afghanistan – but they had never heard anything like this: Richard Burton in one ear, Tom Jones in the other, stereophonically balanced by wild Welsh wit.

I first met Stuart about ten years ago. It was St George's Day, and, understandably, I was gutted. (Okay, every saint has his day, but this halo-headed goody-goody stuck a giant syringe into the arse of the only Welsh animal that smoked – the Red Dragon.) Reading about Stuart and the other two Stereophonics in the music press had given me the idea that they were three straight, non-smoking, possibly teetotal, well-behaved Valleys kids earnestly dedicating themselves to bringing certain aspects of Welsh culture to the English and other immigrants. Soon they would be shagging groupies behind slagheaps of sheep shit, and it would all be over. I had it wrong. So had Stuart. Reading about me in the music press had given him the impression I was a teetotal, well-over-the-hill hippie, who had progressed from smoking weed to jacking up smack because his lungs had packed up.

We learned that we had much in common. Stuart was born, bred and buttered in a small Welsh village comprising a few pubs, a road and a chapel or two. So was I. Stuart had missed the dance culture. So had I. I had a great excuse: I was banged up in the nick. So did he: the South Wales Valleys had outlawed virtually all music made after 1979. The jukeboxes in the corners of the lounge bars, those mechanical muses that still smoulder in the watering holes of the Rhondda and neighbouring valleys, provided the entire musical repertoire. We both liked AC/DC, Kiss, Rush, Deep Purple, Lynyrd Skynyrd, Guns N' Roses, Led Zeppelin, Credence Clearwater, the Kinks, Stevie Wonder, Rainbow and Bad Company. We both still wear their T-shirts. We both liked getting bladdered. We both liked being caned.

'All right, 'Ow? 'Ow's it going? I thought you would never bloody answer! Shall we have a pint? Let's go to that pub you were on about, that one with a wall that talks in medieval Welsh.'

We went to the Prince of Wales in Kenfig, Wales's most haunted pub. The regulars had seen it all, too. I had brought all sorts of celebrities, from famous film actors to sexy models, to this local pub. None had attracted more than passing glances. They were used to ghosts, for fuck's sake. However, when Stuart walked in, everyone immediately perceived he was one of their own. Within minutes, he was deep in animated jovial discussion with all of them.

When Stuart got too much education to carry on performing and hitting the word around, he embarked upon an extraordinarily successful career of TV and radio presentation. His compassionate, humorous, humble and well-grounded charisma invariably swamped audiences and guests, and his vibrant, impossible-to-dislike personality and unique voice made him an obvious frontman for numerous charitable causes, work that he tenaciously continues.

Stuart is the perfect master, exponent, and representative of 'Wenglish', a deliberately ignored dialect with its own unique vocabulary and consistent grammar, spoken and understood by well over a million people living in the South Wales Valleys. Wenglish began as the *lingua franca* of the mining valleys when they became the favoured destination of economic migrants from countries scattered throughout the world, and persists as a fusion of Welsh intonation with Welsh and immigrant English vocabulary. It's the grafters' Esperanto, the most diplomatic of all tongues. Until Stuart's work on his chat show *Cable TV* for BBC Wales and Kerrang! (the radio channel), Wenglish had not streamed through the airwaves. If I had to choose an ambassador for Wales, I would choose him.

# PROLOGUE

# BACK, CRACK AND THE SACK!

I listened to what Kelly had to say on my mobile phone. I was sitting in the car outside my house in Aberdare, really late one Sunday Night in September of 2003. His words buzzed around the inside of my brain like a swarm of angry bees on amphetamines. I wasn't sure if I was relieved or angry, or both. In any case, it took an age for what he had just said to finally sink in.

All of my life, I had boasted to everyone on the planet about how good Kelly was at telling stories about small-town life through his songs. He was my Welsh Shakespeare, my Tarantino of the Valleys, my little, anecdotal, enlightening Ronnie Corbett with greased-up hair, Levi's and a tight-fitting leather jacket. But his latest well-rehearsed verse left me feeling none of that about him. I muttered something back into the receiver, and a second later the line went dead. I sat motionless for a while watching the drizzle dance on my windscreen.

'You yellow-spined bastard!' I yelled out loud. 'How could you end it like this?' He was supposed to be my best mate and he didn't even have the guts to tell me face to face. He and Richard weren't even in the same country, let alone the same fucking continent, when they decided to let me know I was no longer in the band.

To be quite frank, I had a sneaking feeling a few days before that something wasn't quite right, but the end still came like a kick in the balls from a pair of steel-toecapped boots.

And their timing couldn't have been better, either. I had just flown back from Los Angeles, after having an operation to remove an abscess from my arse the size of a blood orange that would have made Jack the Ripper squeamish, and I was feeling quite awful. Just what best mates are for, right?

'What am I going to say to people?' was the first thought in my overactive mind. 'What am I going to tell my mother?' She would be devastated. She had watched us grow from teenage boys messing about in a garage to becoming one of the biggest bands in the UK. I wondered if I should try to break it to her gently or just come right out and tell her. I pictured myself calling round her house and nonchalantly asking her during a mug of tea and a couple of custard creams, 'Hey, Mum, do you know if there are still jobs going at the chicken factory?'

I needed some time to think about my next move. Thankfully, the only thing Kelly and I had agreed on during the brief phone conversation was that we would keep it to ourselves until they got back from America, and then we would sit down and decide how we were going to break the news of the split to everyone else.

## BACK, CRACK AND THE SACK!

Keep it to ourselves, my arse! You can imagine just how big a prat I felt, when, only two days later while I was in London, my mobile phone rang and Owen Money from BBC Radio Wales was on the line. 'Hi, Stu, what's this about you getting sacked from the band, butt?' He left the question hanging there with just enough rope to allow me to hang myself several times over.

'Don't be so stupid,' I lied. My world was caving in around my head. Or was my head caving in around my world? 'What are you talking about?'

'No, honest butt, I've got the press release in my hand. It's all over the news.'

I was shell-shocked. In my mind I could picture all the people who worked at the radio station crammed into Owen's little booth waiting with bated breath for my reply. I automatically went into defensive mode. 'No, don't be so stupid.'

I could tell by his tone that he knew I was bullshitting. He added slowly, 'But it's been signed by Richard and Kelly, Stu.' Even though there was traffic everywhere as I walked down the busy high street, the silence surrounding me was deafening.

I turned off the phone without explaining. Then the anger kicked in. I was fuckin' tamping: they didn't even have the decency to wait to discuss how we were going to announce my departure. After all the times we had been through – the laughs, the tears, the highs, the lows, the all-night benders and the morning-after hangovers. For probably the first time in my life, I was speechless. I had been there from the start of the roller-coaster ride called the Stereophonics, and now they were suddenly unhitching me from the track, leaving me to ride alone for the first time in over ten years.

I wasn't stupid enough to believe that I had been an angel in the whole affair. In fact, I knew at times I had been the biggest clown in the universe, but I thought they could have at least shown me a little more respect than this. They might have sat down with me and talked it through like old friends.

Later that night, I sat in a bar in Covent Garden all alone. I ordered a bottle of lager and tried to rack my brain as to where it had all gone so wrong.

'Stuart's got a lovely arse … shame about the drumming … ha ha.'

**Liam Gallagher, front man with one of the best rock'n'roll bands in the world, Oasis.**

'When Stuart stayed with me and my wife it was the worse time of my life. I used to wake up in a cold sweat and think it was all one big nightmare that this rock star was living with us. But then I'd hear him rustling about in the spare room and the shivers would race up my spine. If I could have my life all over again, I would want it to be Cable Free.

Only messing, I love him to death…'

**Dewi Pws, actor and comic**

# CHAPTER 1

# COMING ALIVE IN DEADTOWN

**M**y mother used to tell me I was born under a wandering star. My brother, Paul, said I was discovered in a brown paper bag under a large hairdryer in an Afro salon in Pontypridd alongside Tom Jones, Kevin Keegan and Leo Sayer. But, just to put the record straight, I actually arrived in this big bad world on a typically cold, rainy old night in Aberdare General Hospital on 19 May 1970. And, no, the town clock didn't stop dead at that exact moment, never to move again. Birds didn't fly out of the trees and dogs didn't start to howl at the moon, as some people might think. In fact, in the age-old tradition of a typically Welsh working-class way of life, my father kissed my mother and me goodnight, and then rushed straight off to the social club to wet his newborn's large, and rather strange-looking, head.

'It's a boy,' he announced as he strolled into the lounge. 'But I don't think he'll ever win the cutest-baby competition. If he'd been a puppy, we'd have drowned him at birth,' he joked. 'He's got a fine pair of lungs on him, mind.'

My old man was always cracking jokes. He came to life when he was the centre of attention, especially at family functions, where he always got up to do a turn. People still tell me today that my father was hilarious, the life and soul of all the parties.

Before my parents were married, my old man Arthur spent the first part of his working life messing around in the Air Force. His main job was laying out bomb targets for the pilots to blow the shite out of. When he returned home, he got a job as a crane driver in a factory in my hometown. He met my mother during a dance at the Aberdare Welfare Club. She told me she had fallen in love with him at first sight. Not long after that, he asked her to marry him. Love or not, I still think she must have had balls the size of melons to actually say yes, knowing full well that she would suddenly go from Mabel Edwards, to the now-infamous Mabel bloody Cable!

I'm not sure why, but I used to hate her name when I was growing up. When anyone mentioned my mother by both names, it sent a shiver down my spine. 'Oh, it's Mabel Cable's little curly-haired boy,' people would say, and they'd smile at me, except for my uncle, who used to take great pleasure in telling everyone I was the spitting image of Shirley Temple!

Eventually, over time, I grew up and realised it was only a name. In fact, her middle name is Annette and now I often joke with her that it could have been much, much worse. She might have married some bloke with the last name Curtain. Or she could have been one of those poor unfortunate souls landed with a name like Justin Case or Dwayne Pipe, or Albert Hall. What the hell were those parents thinking of when they sentenced their poor, innocent, newborn babes to a lifetime of ridicule? I personally think amusing names should be banned if they're inappropriate, just like weird licence plates.

Anyway, the bizarre thing is that, even today, people say to me, especially after a few drinks, 'Stuart, do you mind if I ask you something?' Normally I shrug my shoulders, smile weakly and wait for the big sixty-four-thousand-dollar question, which I always think will be something like, 'Why did you get booted out of one of the biggest bands in the UK?' But unbelievably, eight times out of ten, they look me in the eye and shuffle awkwardly from foot to foot before muttering, 'Is your mother *really* called Mabel Cable?'

It's as if they think she's some kind of alien or a name-rhyming serial killer who finds extreme pleasure in strangling her victims before carving her initials into their chest: 'MC was here!'

My parents were happily married until my old man died in 1980. He was only 49 years old. He dropped dead cleaning the snooker table in the social club. It happened on a Wednesday night. He had hurried home from work and straight down the club to get everything ready for a big tournament. Apparently, he was wiping specks of dust off the green cloth while telling the regulars a joke, when he had a massive heart attack and collapsed onto the floor. At first no one moved, they thought he was just fucking about. It must have been a bit like the night the comic legend Tommy Cooper died while on stage. I was told all the regulars just stared at him, waiting for him to get back up. When they realised something was really wrong, a guy called Richard Geek resuscitated him for a brief moment, only for another attack to choke the life out of him for ever.

Up to that point, my life had been quite normal – as normal as that of a young boy living in a small, compact village like Cwmaman could be, anyway. But that day changed everything for me. I didn't really know my old man that well. I was only 10 and getting to know him wasn't at the top of my priority list. I guess I just wasn't expecting him to die so soon. Anyway, I'm not sure how I felt at the time, but I know it took a while to realise he wouldn't be around any more. I remember at times thinking that it was so unfair that other kids' dads hadn't passed away and mine had.

I remember my mother crying as if there were no tomorrow. As you can imagine, she took the whole situation really badly. The doctor prescribed some medication that turned her into a zombie for a while. Overnight, my easygoing and colourful life seemed to turn dark and gloomy.

I recall the day of the funeral vividly. It was massive, cars and people as far back as the eye could see. The entire passageway and front room were covered in flowers and sadness. My mother was too upset to go, and, for whatever reason, she didn't allow me to go, either. I've never completely forgiven her for that. My brother went alone with the rest of our relatives. It must have been terrible for him. Even to this day, he never mentions my father, or that day.

Paul was a 17-year-old boy, who had his youth snatched away from him overnight. He had to become the head of the household and the father figure. I never really appreciated the responsibility that had been forced on his young shoulders, or the extra pressure I added by being a 10-year-old who was rapidly changing into some kind of loud-mouthed, cocky upstart with werewolf tendencies.

## COMING ALIVE IN DEADTOWN

I refused to listen to him and he would go mad and batter me senseless. I hated him then. I was too young and stupid to realise just how much he had on his plate. It was a time in his life when he should have been given support and guidance rather than having to give it to an ungrateful little brother.

On the occasions when I pushed him too far, my mother would take control of the situation in her own unique way. Normally, she would lose her cool and beat me with her slipper. I swear she was a black belt in slipper combat, a 'Furry Slipper 10 Dan' in a cotton nightdress and plastic curlers. On a bad day, she would turn into a cross between Bruce Lee, Jackie Chan and Billy the Kid. I'm sure she must have gone to some sort of foot weapon classes for years to get that good. She could remove her slipper, aim, fire, strike and have it back on her foot within a blink of an eyelash. She could wallop me from twenty-five paces away.

When I started to get older and too tough for her soft-leather-footwear assaults, she would reach for the poker and try to whack me on the shin with it. She only did it once and fucking hell, man, it hurt! It was the most painful experience known to man- or boykind, even worse than pulling nose hair. Forget Chinese water torture, the Spanish Inquisition or kneecapping, getting whacked with a poker is top-drawer punishment. Nothing compares to the thud and pain of iron on skin. It's bastard cruel. Even today, whenever I see an open fireplace, I cringe.

It didn't get any easier for my mother, either, even as time passed. I'm just thankful she didn't go the way of other women in similar situations: turning to drink, drugs, or God forbid, 24-hour bingo. No, Mabel managed to pull it all around. Others might disagree, but I think she and my brother did a respectable job of bringing me up. She passed on a decent set of morals and taught me the value of money. From an early age I remember her saying, 'If you can't afford it, don't buy it.' While I watched my mates bury themselves in the debt of cars and lots of other stuff they really didn't need, those words would play out in my head. It really helped me think twice about spending money I didn't have. It still keeps me out of trouble and debt to this day – although I will admit that, when I did start to earn big bucks with the band, I probably purchased more signed photographs and death certificates of my heroes than I really needed. But, hey, you gotta have a passion for something.

I still miss my dad, every day of my life. It's tough not being able to share with him all the special places I have had the privilege to go, and the important people I've had the honour to meet – especially knowing that he would have appreciated it more than anyone that I know. He was a huge sports fan: he played rugby for the local team until he was 41 years old, which at that time was quite an achievement. It would have been great to have had him there when we played at what used to be the Morfa Stadium near Swansea (more on that venue later), and met the great Gareth Edwards, or to have had him with me when I bumped into other sporting legends like Barry John, JPR and Gerald Davies. And I know he would have loved every minute of my friendship with Scott Gibbs and Jonathan Davies. I know this is a strange and rather selfish thing to say, but I think he was a twat to go and die like that. Why couldn't he have been there for me, like Kelly's and Richard's fathers? We could have enjoyed it all together. Okay, maybe not all of it: I don't think he would have appreciated some of the darker sides of the rock'n'roll lifestyle, but he would definitely have liked the music, the people and the drink.

I'm convinced he's still with me in spirit, though. Years ago, I got dragged to see a clairvoyant by a girlfriend who was into all the spiritualist stuff. At the time I didn't believe in any of it; I thought it was all complete nonsense. I sat there in a small room in Newport, Gwent, giving curt answers and just nodding my head to the weird-looking woman with a tea towel round her head. At first she was very ropey, to say the least. It reminded me of the film *Ghost*. I was dying to laugh and piss off to the pub. But after a while she got my attention when she went into a strange trance and informed me there was a rather talkative woman called Joan there to see me. Like a complete knob, I looked round the room expecting to see someone sitting in the corner. My Auntie Joan had died not long after my father and I was told, and remember, that she was the gobbiest motherfucker who'd ever lived. She could talk a glass eye to sleep! The clairvoyant then said something that made the hairs on the back of my neck stand on end. She told me there was someone called Arthur standing behind my aunt. She described my father to a T. Apparently, he was trying to tell me something, but my auntie kept interrupting.

'Shut the fuck up, Joan!' I found the voice in my head screaming out. 'What did he say?' I asked the psychic.

She looked at me and whispered, 'He told me he was watching over your shoulder when you played Glastonbury, and he was there at some of the other gigs.'

It was real spooky. I felt like crying. Shivers raced up my spine. I wanted to know more, but she said they had gone. Then she told me there was someone else who wanted to speak.

'Fucking hell!' I thought. 'I hope it's Bonnie Scott or Keith Moon.' I sat on the edge of my seat.

But, instead, she told me something that I have never mentioned to anyone before. She said there was a woman in the room who was the mother of someone called Jools.

I stared at the woman. 'Jools who?' I asked innocently.

She continued, 'Jools Holland. It's his mother and she wants to speak to him.' The clairvoyant looked at me. 'She said you know him.'

'Well?' I shrugged my shoulders. I wasn't sure where this was all leading to.

'She would like you to phone him now.' I felt everyone's eyes staring at me.

'And tell him what?' I asked. In my mind I played out the scene. 'Hi, Jools, Stuart here. Thought the New Year's Eve show was great this year. Oh, and by the way, I'm in Newport with a spiritualist at the moment and she just happens to have your dead mother floating around the room. Do you fancy a chat, or should I take a message?' I shook my head, thanked her, paid, and then got up and left.

I rushed home to tell my mother about the experience with my father and my Auntie Joan. She dismissed it, saying it was stupid and preposterous. And that was that. She never mentioned it again and I've never been back to see another psychic since, although I do hope she was right about my father looking over my shoulder.

Besides those memories of my father's death, my memories of growing up in the village are of a rather laid-back existence, discounting the occasional brother-beating and slipper-whacking. Cwmaman is in a valley surrounded by mountainside and plenty of wilderness. There is only one way in, and one way out. Some would say one way in and no way out. It was a close-knit community. Everyone knew everyone's business and what they didn't know they would, of course, make up. It was, and still is, a great place for someone like Kelly to get plenty of material to fuel his immense writing talents. He people-watched all the time and there were some really weird and wonderful characters on every street corner or slumped into pints of beer in the Ivy Bush to watch. Towns and villages are built on characters and Cwmaman has enough characters to build skyscraper after skyscraper, and still have a couple left over to erect a decent-sized garage.

It had its own feel to it, its own laws. There were no outsiders or strangers hanging around. It was a place where you could leave your back door open. Besides the odd grizzly bear wandering in from time to time from the forest, pissed up on cider looking for some food, there was never really anything to fear. No one worried about their things getting stolen or their kids being kidnapped, not like today. I know that sounds *so* old-fashioned, but that's the way it was. And, by the way, the grizzly bears were a piece of piss. We just ganged up on them and ran them out of town with their tails planted firmly between their legs. Just jokin'.

My fondest recollection of my childhood was hanging around the open-air swimming pool opposite Glanaman Road, where Kelly and I lived. We would spend all our summer sitting by the water, listening to music and trying to look cool in front of the girls. To me there was no better place in the world to grow up.

## DEMONS AND COCKTAILS

The only part of my youth I really hated was being sheep-dipped in a vat of poor comprehensive-school education. I hated school with a passion. I couldn't see the point in it, maybe because I was so awful at it. The only things I was good at were metalwork and bunking off lessons. I later passed a GCSE in both subjects. I also got pretty good at sniffing the occasional odd substances behind the sports hall now and then, as well. When I was around 15, sniffing PR spray (the sort used by athletes) became the new teenage craze – in Aberdare anyway. Of course I was the first in the queue to try it out. Up to that point I had never smoked, drank or done drugs of any kind, not even sniffed glue. Not sure what made me start then. I think I just needed something to get me through my school days, or perhaps I had to have something to help me make sense of what the fuck antilogarithms were. Obviously, it didn't help me in that area, because I still don't know what the fuck they are. If anyone can tell me what they're used for, or if they have actually used them in the real world, please send me a postcard marked for the attention of Stuart, the house with the two big dogs, Wales.

Anyway, I couldn't wait for dinnertime, when me and the gang, the mental heads from nearby Abercwmboi, would sneak over into the field opposite. We would spray the substance onto the sleeves of our jumpers and then inhale. It was magic. It would hit me like a bolt of lightning. The weird thing is, because this stuff is used by athletes to spray on aches and strains, whenever I got high I would lie back on the grass and picture rugby players running out onto the field. Later on in life when I went to watch Wales playing at the Millennium Stadium, I would automatically imagine fifteen cans of PR spray running out in red jerseys. How fucked up is that? That's what a comprehensive education does for you.

My school, Blaengwawr Comprehensive, was a right crazy old place. It was the last chance saloon for many pupils. They used to send all the problem kids from the other areas there. It became the Alcatraz of comprehensive schools, famous throughout the Valleys; all nutcases lead to Blaengwawr.

I still recall the register in class each morning.

'Cable?'

'Here, Miss.'

'Capone?'

'Here.'

'The Kray Twins?'

'I'm here, Miss, but Reggie's ill today – something wrong with his brain.'

I'm only messing, but there were some real lunatics there who had definitely sniffed too many weird substances. I would love to know where they all ended up – probably A&R people or newspaper journalists.

I was no saint, either, mind. My school reports throughout the years followed very much the same theme, but with slightly different wording: Stuart's head is elsewhere. He must try harder. He's got it in him, but he must stop talking. So, basically, all my years of education can be summed up in six words: Stuart is a chopsey twat. Or is that five? Told you I was bad. Anyway, I think all the teachers, plus the headmaster and the dinner ladies, took great pride in signing each and every report.

'So what do you want to be when you grow up, Stuart?' they would ask me. How the fuck was I supposed to know? I hadn't discovered the drums yet. I was thinking maybe chief quality inspector for PR Spray Company, or head scout for bunking officers. That would have suited me right down to the ground. But I really had no idea. I just knew there was no way I'd ever let myself get stuck working in the furnace plant that polluted the Valleys, or go to work down a mine. The money was great, but not good enough to live life in black clothes and with a scarred face. Besides, can you imagine what I would have had to spend on shampoo and conditioner to get all that soot out of my hair?

By the end of school, I had started to get involved quite seriously in various bands, and somehow I just knew I was destined to ride on the train to stardom. So, like all good rock stars down the ages, I followed my instincts and became an apprentice carpenter, which was even more ironic considering I liked only metalwork.

It was really boring and I packed it in when I realised I was nothing more than a cheap form of labour who spent entirely too much time digging holes in the ground. When someone finally told me I could make a lot more money making PVC windows, I went to work in a factory fabricating plastic windows in Hirwaun. It actually wasn't too bad and I did quite well. After I had been there a while, the foreman asked me if I fancied becoming a window fitter. 'Fuckin' hell!' I thought, as he issued me with my own van and tool belt. 'I've made it. Today, I'm fabricating double-glazed sash windows for a semidetached in Rhigos; tomorrow, fuck knows. If I'm really lucky, I'll be erecting a twelve-foot conservatory with a patio door and new PVC guttering in the posh part of town. The world is my ostrich.' Sorry, oyster.

## COMING ALIVE IN DEADTOWN

I went out on the road with a guy called Terry Price, who was completely bonkers but I had a great time. We stretched the meaning of the word 'work' to its limit; we were always thinking of ways to make our lives easier. Once, we did a small job in a place called Mountain Ash and we knew that, if we finished early and went back to the depot, we would probably be given another job to do. So we decided halfway through the job to take a little nap, and we fell asleep on the owner's bed. About two hours later, she woke us up and offered us a cup of tea and a plate of biscuits. That's the great thing about Welsh people.

Another time I recall we were in Merthyr Vale fitting some windows in a couple's bedroom. Terry found a photo album on top of the wardrobe. Being the pair of nosy fuckers that we were, we had a gander. We hit the jackpot. It was full of photos of the wife, who was quite smart for someone from Merthyr. Well, she had her own teeth and her tattoos were spelt right, anyway. She was topless on various beaches in Spain. There were loads of them taken at different time periods down the years. Terry and I stood on the scaffold lusting at them as if we hadn't seen a pair of tits in our lives. We were both drooling like a couple of hungry bulldogs until a big gust of wind blew the photos everywhere. We spent hours trying to rearrange the pictures in the original order by checking the shade of the woman's tan, to make sure she didn't find out – and, more crucially, tell her husband, who was a right big, mean bastard.

Not surprisingly, I got made redundant shortly after that, and sadly had to give back the van and the fucking tool belt. I was gutted. After that I decided I would do what most of the other 'sane' blokes in Cwmaman did: I signed on the dole and started

**13**

hobbling. I would do anything for a few bucks: digging, picking weeds, painting; I would talk myself into most fiddles. But the money was ropey and after a short while people realised my teachers were spot on: I was just a chopsey twat. I was crap at doing everything. My hobbling days ended rather quickly.

My brother then got me a proper job once again in the factory where he worked, making filing cabinets. I worked on a fly press, which is a big metal machine that squashes material into different shapes and sizes. I must have squashed a billion pieces of metal in my time. It was mind-numbing. I was like a one-armed monkey in some kind of freak zoo with a DON'T FEED THE STUART sign above my head. If I was really lucky and made my number, I would get an extra £3.75 a week bonus.

The problem was, I didn't care about hitting my number so I could get the bonus. By that time I wanted to hit drum skins, not make indents in drawer runners. My brother worked on the same machine as Kelly's old man, Oscar. They used to pour material into a large hopper and sit down talking throughout the shift while I fly-pressed away like some prisoner serving out his sentence.

I hated it so much that I convinced some of the other workers that we should start a union. For a very short while I was 'the Arthur Scargill of Fur Steel'. (Remember Arthur Scargill? He was the bloke from Yorkshire who led the miners back in the days when they went on strike big time.) Luckily, I got sacked. Inside, I was pleased to get out, although my brother was pissed off. My mother told me I should get my head out of the clouds, start acting my age and stop dreaming of something I would never become.

'I'll show you lot!' I told myself, and got a job delivering school dinners to comprehensive schools in the area. I can only imagine what my old headmaster thought on seeing me saunter through the gates in my green trousers, white shirt and a baseball cap worn back to front. He probably phoned the police or reached for a gun. On second thoughts, he probably wasn't surprised at all that I had lived right up to his expectations.

My first day was a disaster. I thought I was so cool that I wheel-spun out of the car park where the food was prepared. Before I got to the first school, all the beans I was delivering, had tipped over in the back of the van. It was like a raging sea of orange muck. I didn't want the kids to call me a wanker for spoiling their dinner – well, not on my first day, anyway – so I drove back to the kitchen and took some more beans down on my lunch break.

It was a crazy place to work. There were 4 guys delivering and 24 women cooking the food. They used to tease me. 'Hey, Curly, when you're a rock star will you come back and see us?' And then they would try to grab my arse.

On the day I walked in and handed in my notice, the supervisor asked, 'What's happened? Got a job in Tesco, have you?'

'No, we've just signed a record deal,' I answered, trying to sound cool.

'Oh, that's nice,' she said, dismissively. 'Probably see you back in a few weeks, then.'

'I don't think so,' I replied, resisting the urge to brag to her that we had just pocketed £250,000. Or, to be more precise, we put £247,000 in our joint bank account and £3,000 in cash in our back pockets, which I will explain all about later.

'Stuart was confident from the very beginning that they would be famous. He practised every day with Kelly and Richard, which I really didn't mind because at least I knew where he was. I knew he wasn't out muggin' or druggin' like some boys in the town.'

**Mabel Cable, Stuart's mum and 'Black Slipper 10 Dan' expert**

## CHAPTER 2

# THE TEENAGE
# KICK YEARS

**A**s I mentioned earlier, Cwmaman was a great place to grow up, and hanging out round the swimming pool was the centre of our little world. I remember one of my early encounters with a rather naïve Kelly Jones. He was a couple of years younger than I was. I was about 13 and he must have been around 9. I'm not sure if it was the extra helping of strawberry sauce on my 99 ice cream, or just the devilry inside, that made me decide to teach him the art of swearing. I started him off on low-level stuff, like *shit* and *bollocks*, and, as the afternoon progressed, I introduced him to the queen of all swearwords, *Fuck*, with a capital *F*. At first, he wouldn't say it. But, trust my luck, when he finally did let loose and let loose loudly, my mother came round the corner and heard him.

'Kelly!' she cried. 'That's a very naughty word. Who taught you to say something like that?'

I knew what was coming and tried my best to sneak away

quietly as he innocently raised his arm and pointed right at me. At that moment, it was as if the entire village had stopped to stare at me. I felt like a criminal, a desperado, and to make matters worse, the F-word accidentally slipped out of my mouth as well.

'Stuart!' my mother screamed and automatically reached down for her slipper. Thankfully, we were outside so she had her boots on. Since it would have taken her an age to untie them, I escaped the deadly shoe to the head. But I didn't escape entirely: instead of a beating I ended up grounded for a week, which was probably worse. I sat upstairs in the confines of my bedroom moping about like a prisoner in a cell while everyone else lazed by the pool, eating ice cream and swearing like fucking troopers.

Years later when we were famous-ish and we won the Brit Award for the much-coveted Best Newcomer, I remember Kelly whispering to me while we nervously sat waiting for the result, 'If we win, no swearing.'

'You cheeky cunt! Of *course* I'm not going to swear,' I said – and I winked at him and smirked back.

We all held our breath as Jo Whiley was about to announce the winner.

'And the winner is … ' – the pause lasted a million years – 'the Stereophonics!' The words echoed round the vast hall, the lights shone on us and everyone turned to stare.

'*Fuckin' hell!*' I gulped.

We rushed up onto the stage as if they were going to give it to someone else. All our plans of strolling up, lips curled and looking all cool like the previous winners, Oasis, were discarded. My heart was beating. The mixture of beer and whisky pumped around my veins. Kelly's warning of no swearing was racing around my head.

I thought I would crack under the pressure. I felt like a Tourette sufferer on the verge of a ranting fit.

Up on stage, Kelly grabbed the statue, which I thought was quite brave, considering it was almost as big as he was. Then, for whatever reason, he suddenly blurted out to the British public, 'It's about time we got some fucking recognition!' And then we walked off.

I was shocked. I'm not sure if he planned it, if this was the start of his metamorphosis into a full-blown rock star, or if Chubby Brown helped him to write his acceptance speech. In a way I know what he meant and how he felt. We had been struggling our bollocks off without much support from the likes of Radio 1, and I believe all the pent-up frustration inside him just came pouring out.

Believe it or not, I honestly feel the hue and cry concerning his swearing rant overshadowed our actual achievement. My mother still mentions it to this day. I'm also sure this was one of the reasons why some sections of the music press turned against us. But, then again, I think there were many other reasons they did that!

When I got kicked out of the band, I couldn't help but picture Kelly standing, all puppy-eyed, in front of the press blurting out his rather biased side of the story of why they had sacked me. I honestly thought he would explain that I was really to blame for his outburst at the Brit Awards, since it was me, nasty Stuart Cable, who had taught him to say the word *fuck* in the first place, all those years ago. I always knew it would end up being my fault somewhere down the fucking line.

# DEMONS AND COCKTAILS

I really started to get into music in my teens. I think it was because my brother was always listening to rock music and it offered me an escape from life. Apparently, Kelly's and Richard's brothers were the same; a lot of their rock influences rubbed off on them as well. Thinking back now, I recall that everyone in Cwmaman was into rock music, really. It was the heavy-metal equivalent of the Stepford Wives. I think every man, woman and child could recite the words to 'Paranoid' by Black Sabbath like robots, and could play Deep Purple's riff to 'Smoke on the Water' on one-string guitars.

Strangely enough, there just weren't any punks, skinheads or Mods to be found. It was a village built on a foundation of hard rock with pillars of fifteen-minute guitar solos and big-drum intros. Many of my non-Cwmaman friends often say that Cwmaman is so behind the times that 'God Save the Queen' by the Sex Pistols won't get to Number 1 in the music charts until the year 2012. I disagree. I think the only chance of its ever reaching Number 1 in Cwmaman is if Ozzy Osbourne remakes it with Angus Young on guitar.

Because of my brother, I grew up on a diet of the Eagles, Genesis, Bob Dylan and Neil Young. My appearance mirrored that of my heroes: desert boots, checked shirts and Wranglers. I even wore a denim jacket with the sleeves cut off over my leather coat. I remember it had AC/DC and Rush patches on the back. I thought I was the kiddy until, one day, one of my mates turned up with Led Zeppelin hand-embroidered on the back of his Levi jacket. It was fucking ace. I was so envious. Trust his mother to be good at sewing while mine was shit hot at beating me half to death with her slipper.

It wasn't until the day I saw AC/DC performing on *The Old Grey Whistle Test*, though, that the light came on in my head. That was when I knew exactly what I wanted to be. Music had entered my blood; rhythm had engulfed my soul. I wanted to be a rock star.

My first attempt at stardom was singing with a band called Nail Bombs. Eat your heart out, Elvis; be scared, Bonnie: Cable was coming. True to form, I was fucking terrible. And to add insult to injury, I looked even worse. My shirt kept falling over my shoulder, exposing white bare flesh. Last year, some girl found a picture of the gig and used the photo of me in a quiz in my local pub. No one knew who it was. Someone thought I was Janice Joplin during her ugly period. One regular actually got sick, while the landlord of the pub joked about putting the picture above the mantelpiece to keep the kids from going near the fire.

I tried lead guitar next. I was crap at that, too. When people are bad at playing sport, they are told they have two left feet. When I played guitar, I had eight left fingers and two handicapped thumbs. I snapped three strings in my first strum. I looked around at what else I could do. Bass guitar looked too boring for me and definitely wouldn't suit my outgoing personality. Drumming was the only thing left, and it looked quite easy.

'I'm going to bash drums.'

My brother was my saviour. He was wonderful. I asked him if he could lend me £60 to buy my first set.

'No problem,' he said and got me the dosh straightaway.

Fair play to him. I had been a little bastard to him for most of my teenage life, but he didn't think twice about giving it to me.

Now that's what being a brother is all about, and come to think of it, I still haven't paid him back.

I was so excited when I assembled them in my bedroom. They were a Premier Olympic kit: yellow, the same colour as the set Ringo Starr used. I was over the moon. I played them morning, noon and night until my neighbours, who were normally very nice, knocked on the door to have a chat with my mother. She was always threatening to get rid of my drums and put me out of her house. We eventually came to a compromise: I could play as much as I wanted between the hours of nine in the morning and nine at night.

It changed my life. I practised every day for about a year. I bashed them in my bedroom, out in the garden, in the front room. I would tape my favourite songs and just play along to them. It felt exactly like the guy in the film *The Commitments*, drumming away in the pawn shop. I dreamt about drumming while I was in school and then later when I went to work; I couldn't wait to get home to play them. They made me feel special. I didn't need anyone or anything when I was playing drums. As soon as I got behind that snare, I turned into a different person. I was confident, I was in control, no longer the idiot hiding at the back of the class. For the first time, I knew what I wanted in my life – and I was getting better and better at it every day. Drumming was my new drug and I wanted to inject a piece of the rock'n'roll lifestyle into my veins. Getting the fix of fans, drink, women and everything else I knew came along with success was my motivation.

One day, Kelly knocked on my door. I still hadn't fully forgiven him for getting me into trouble with the swearing incident.

'Hey, fancy having a knock together?' he asked. 'I've heard you playing drums.' He was holding up a guitar that his father had bought him about the same time as I got my kit.

'Okay,' I replied excitedly. To be honest, I had become a bit drum-stir-crazy playing along by myself, so this was just the opportunity I was looking for. And I suspected my mother was pleased I was at least out of the house for a while.

And that was how it all started. But it certainly wasn't a straightforward journey from that initial meeting to finally reaching the destination known as the Stereophonics. There were a couple of twists and turns and the odd pothole waiting to trip us up along the way, as with most bands starting out. It's actually quite amazing that we made it, really.

We started to practise in Kelly's old man's garage. After a while Nicholas Geek joined us on guitar. And then Kelly knew a couple of other guys to add to the ranks: Paul Rosser on bass and Chris Davies on keyboard. I think I was the one who suggested Kelly should be the lead singer because his old man, Oscar, used to be a very good singer in the sixties. He had supported Roy Orbison and others, and had also made several records. I thought that if he could do it, so too could Kelly.

We started off playing stuff by Zeppelin and Van Halen, and, since I was the oldest and the loudest in the band, we also had a go at some songs by Rush, who were my favourite band. For some reason we also did a bizarre cover version of 'Baker Street' by Gerry Rafferty, which I think was Oscar's suggestion.

Oscar was always popping down to the garage to give us advice. At first, we all listened to him intently, but after a while it started to get on everyone's tits, even Kelly's. I think his old man was trying to relive past glory days through us.

'This is how you should do it; this is what you should try to sing. No, don't bring the drums in there – wait for the bass to kick in.'

Looking back now, I'm reminded of that annoying nosy neighbour character on *Harry Enfield and Chums*. 'Only me … I don't think you wanted to do it like that.'

But, to be fair to him, he did teach us a lot. The most important thing he told us was to play for the song, not the individual part of it. And that it should be the melody line first and foremost, and that everything else is there to support it. I think it's a piece of advice that all bands, famous or not, should always remember.

When we started to write our own stuff, we made a cheap demo, which was really exciting at that age. I was about 16 and had just started the apprentice carpenter's job. The demo was shite, but I didn't care; I had been bitten by the bug. We played a few gigs under the name of Zephyr, which went quite well. Then Kelly went on holiday and we played a gig without him. It was a chance to earn a couple of quid and get some more live practice under our belt. But neither Kelly nor his old man saw it like that. They were pissed off that we had done the show without him, so they picked up Kelly's ball and left the band.

'What a childish little twat!' I thought. 'Who the fuck does he think he is, anyway, Frank Sinatra?' We didn't talk for two years. Not a single word. And we lived on the same fucking street.

So Zephyr had crashed big time into the ditch on the first bend. Kelly, Paul and Chris formed an R&B band called Silent Runner. I grew my hair even bigger, squeezed into a pair of spandex pants and a glittery top, put on some black eyeliner and became the drummer in a glam-rock band aptly named King Catwalk.

We were a cross between Poison, Mötley Crüe and, unfortunately, a little too much Spinal Tap. For some obscure reason, we played most of our gigs up in the North of England. I'm still not sure why. It wasn't as if the people there were into that type of music more than those in any other part of the country. In fact, most of the gigs we played were in front of four or five people. I think it was because we looked so ridiculous when we came out on stage that we subconsciously decided to gig as far as possible away from where we lived.

It was gruesome at times. There's nothing worse, or funnier, than trying to get ready in a dressing room the size of a toilet, with five guys with larger-than-life hairdos covered in lacquer, wearing platform boots. It was a fuckin' safety hazard for starters: one match would have ignited the lot of us. And perishing in some bizarre backstage fire accident was probably the only way we would ever have ended up famous, anyway: 'Here lies the singed hair of King Catwalk – RIP. God forgive them – they know not what they did.'

I got sacked, which was okay because, unlike the rest of the band, I was still trying to hold down a proper job, and travelling through the night to get back home was taking its toll. I really didn't believe the band were destined for bigger things than playing in grotty clubs, anyway, even if the boys thought and acted as if they were on the verge of becoming big rock stars. And they were more interested in getting laid than putting in the work. It was all about how many girls they had shagged rather than the quality of the material.

So, I ended up band-less yet again, but this time I was more determined than ever to make a living doing what I loved. Then, a few weeks later, the hand of fate decided it was time to help me out a little. I was on a bus and saw Kelly standing at the bus stop. I waved at him and he waved back. It was the first contact we had in years. Two weeks later, I was drunk in the Ivy Bush and he came in with Emma, his girlfriend. We started talking and agreed to give the band another go.

'But I'm not playing any R&B stuff,' I told him, which was a bit cheeky since I had just left King of Crap-talk. 'I'd rather do our own stuff.'

He agreed.

I told him I had a great album by a band called the Tragically Hip, a group from Canada, that I wanted him to listen to. He loved it. They wrote songs about small-town lives and stories, which of course turned out to be a massive inspiration for our first album. Later on in our lives, we became good mates with the band and stayed with them a few times in Canada.

One of the first roadblocks to our stardom came when a girl I had a fling with back in the village told me she was pregnant. She was a hell of a sexy girl, very hot, but I couldn't believe she was up the duff. My hopes of becoming a rock star seemed dashed as I imagined myself living in a council flat, wearing a white string vest with five kids, two dogs, a gamy rabbit and a one-way ticket to the social club every afternoon, all because I had a couple of nights of passion in the back of my van. Trust my bloody luck! Thankfully, it all ended up as a false alarm, which was lucky for me in more ways than one.

I was excited again at the prospect of playing with Kelly. We started jamming and invited a boy called Mark Everett to play bass. We were getting really good and Kelly was starting to write our songs. Then Mark went on holiday for two weeks, just when we were beginning to gain some momentum. We weren't going behind Mark's back, but we wanted to carry on rehearsing, so Kelly asked Richard if he fancied helping us out.

I knew Richard from afar and hadn't seen him for a while. I didn't even know he played an instrument. From what I remembered of him, he was a bit of a handful; his entire family were. He had been in trouble with the cops for nicking cars and some other stuff. But I was shocked when he turned up. He was cool as fuck: long hair, good-looking. He had the Axl Rose appearance: tattoos on his arms and his name on his neck. He wore his guitar low down like Sid Vicious, but, unlike the punk-rock star, Richard could actually play his instrument.

We played a few songs and, during a fag break, I told Kelly that I thought he was the one for us. No disrespect to Mark – I loved him to bits – but I felt the band needed the right look as well as the correct sound, and it just felt so right as the three of us bashed out songs all afternoon. We asked Richard if he wanted to be in and he agreed. Then we had to deal with the difficult situation of telling a suntanned and refreshed Mark on his return that he was out. It was a tough call but sometimes you just need to go with your gut.

Funny thing is, after that I don't think anyone in the band had the nerve to go on holiday again. As a matter of fact, I had a terrible fear that my mother would one day come up trumps on the bingo and come home to tell me she had booked the family to go away on a five-star, all-inclusive holiday to Jamaica.

'Sorry, Mam, I'll think I'll pass, unless you take Kelly and Richard as well.' It's funny how your mind works.

---

**MY TOP FIVE MUSICAL INFLUENCES**

AC/DC: The first rock band I was ever exposed to by my brother. They are still a big influence on me.

LED ZEPPELIN: No need for words – brilliant, simply brilliant.

THE TRAGICALLY HIP: First got into them when I was 21. They are great storytellers and became a big influence on the Phonics' first album and the way Kelly still writes his songs.

RUSH: Still my favourite band of all time. Thirty years on and still the tightest band in rock'n'roll.

BLACK SABBATH: I was really into them for a while. I wanted to be Ozzy – but at the time everyone did.

---

# CHAPTER 3

# IT'S A KIND OF TRAGIC (LOVE COMPANY)

After Richard came on board, we played as a three-piece band for a while. We became known as the Tragic Love Company after we decided to merge the names of three of our major rock-band influences at the time: the Tragically Hip, Mother Love Bone and Bad Company. Looking back now, I think we should have played around with the name a bit more: Bad Hip Bone or Mother's Bad Hip, or maybe Tragically Bad Mother, might have sounded a lot cooler. Okay, maybe not.

We also started to take what we did a lot more seriously. We practised hard every day; we really went for it. We ate, slept, drank and shat rock music. Many said that I was the main energy and drive alongside Kelly's obvious writing talent and Richard's looks and composure.

The band became my 24-hour-a-day drug, my craving. I knew as soon as we hit the first note together that we were going to be something special. Everything just clicked: the music, the company, the humour. We were the three fucking musical musketeers: Athos, Porthos and the little intense one!

Some people in Cwmaman didn't think we would ever get anywhere in the music world. 'You're wasting your time, boys,' we were told a million times. 'No one ever makes it from places like this. Only *proper* bands from *proper* places like London get famous.'

What the fuck did they mean by 'proper bands'? I couldn't understand it. We *were* a fucking proper band. But, in everyone else's eyes, we were just the little kids from next door messing about playing jokey tunes.

I guess that's just a typical Welsh approach to life in general, though. As a nation, we are often too afraid to look over the wall, let alone climb over it and see what might be there on the other side. It upsets me sometimes to think how small-minded we can be.

Our whole attitude regarding people from Wales who have become famous is terrible. Take one of our biggest stars in the world, Mr Tom Jones. I don't think we realise just how big Tom Jones is, and what he means to the country. If you go anywhere in the States and say you are from Wales, 95 per cent of the time Americans won't have any idea where that is. But mention it as the place where Tom comes from and their eyes light up. Ask someone in Wales about Tom, and you'll get the same standard reply: 'Tom – he sang in our club before he was famous and he was so bad we threw him off during the interval. He was crap – and the bastard pinched the Christmas turkey.' Does that sum us up, or what?

While Richard and I were getting better and tighter at playing our instruments, Kelly was busy writing songs, and he didn't have to look far for inspiration. At the time, there was a major scandal in the village that threatened to rock its foundations to the core. The tight-knit community was split wide open the day a guy called Billy Dunn was accused of sexually assaulting two schoolgirls in the changing rooms of the local boys' club. It was the biggest controversy ever to hit the village, and was of course the basis for the story captured perfectly by Kelly in the song, 'A Thousand Trees'. I always remember him playing it for me for the first time ever. I sat on my settee while he strummed it on an acoustic guitar in my front room. It was at that moment I realised he was a fucking genius. Kelly Einstein Jones. The way he could take gossip or a local phrase, like 'check my eyelids for holes', and then mould it into a timeless classic song was fucking brilliant. It's an incredible skill that he has. He was able to create songs that would be sung by thousands of fans at our concerts down the years. It's unbelievable. I felt like hugging him when he had finished. I could tell instantly it was a hit in the making. It was a right *proper* fucking song.

Anyway, back to Billy Dunn. He was a football legend in my village. He ran the local boys' club football team. He was a really big noise, the Alf Ramsey of Cwmaman. He trained every single boy down the ages for, like, a million years. He knew everyone's name, position, strengths and weaknesses. I was convinced he had actually invented soccer. But, when the two girls rushed home to tell their parents what he had done to them, it divided the entire village in two, just as religious hatred divides Glasgow on the day of an Old Firm game.

In the Top Club, supporters of Billy would all gather in one corner, while the anti-Billy crew sat in the other. There was lots of yelling and harsh words spoken, and every now and then the odd fight would break out. Over the main gates of the small football field there was an arch in commemoration of Billy's years of service in the community. It was similar to soccer manager Bill Shankly's gates in Liverpool, but on a much smaller and cheaper scale. It was erected to show appreciation for Billy's commitment to the kids and what he believed in. I know from bitter experience how tough it is playing sport in a valley where it never stops raining. So, to be fair to Billy, spending most of his life standing on the sidelines just watching youngsters in the pissing rain was a testament to his dedication and passion. Anyway, the arch was ripped down and destroyed one night. Then Billy's picture was removed, on request, from the wall in the club. This caused the tensions to really mount. Arguments as to whether he was innocent or guilty, or whether his photo should be put back up or not, went on constantly. Even to this day, the arguments about the photo still rage on.

The whole situation was ugly. I have never known the place to be so hostile. He pleaded not guilty, but he ended up getting convicted of the crime and went to prison. I'm really not sure if he did it or not. I know he was a sandwich short of a picnic, as they say, but I'm still split about the incident. Who knows?

During the whole dramatic affair, the band decided we needed a second guitar player. Kelly wasn't great at solos and mainly stuck to chords. We knew we needed something to beef up the sound, so we brought in Simon Collier on lead. He didn't last long, although he later became Kelly's guitar technician when we got big, and he's still a very good friend of mine today. We drafted in another Richard Jones, but he didn't last either. Then we had a guy from Merthyr called Glenn Hyde. I really liked Glenn. We clicked straightaway. He had a great sense of humour, very Monty Python-ish, very quick-witted. He would stay over at my house on occasions and we always enjoyed a few drinks; he was probably a better musician than all of us put together, and his voice complemented Kelly's extremely well.

Things were going splendidly when, for whatever reason, one night he phoned to tell me he was leaving the band. He wanted to do something else. Six months later we signed a record deal. I felt so sorry for him. He was our Pete Best, the fifth Beatle. Maybe one day someone will make a film about his story: *The Fourth Phonic – The Glenn Hyde Story*. I just hope they get someone dashing such as Ioan Gruffudd to play the part of me, but, knowing my luck, it will probably be Johnny Vegas on acid in a three-foot wig and a nose extension.

I always wonder what the band would have been like if Glenn had stayed. He added a lot to the group and he was a really good songwriter, like Kelly. It would have been interesting. He and Kelly could have been the next famous songwriting team, right up there with Jagger and Richards, Lennon and McCartney, Chas and Dave.

On our third album, *Just Enough Education to Perform*, we were looking for someone to play the harmonic on the last song, 'Rooftop'. I phoned Glenn and asked him if he wanted to help us out. He came to the studio and we had a great time. He's a talented bloke and I wish him the very best in his life.

After Glenn, we agreed to stick to a three-piece band. All the changes in personnel were causing too much disruption. During those early days, we played wherever we could. It was a bit of a circus. We played in some right shit halls, often without anyone there to watch us. We would be doing our best to impress an audience made up of one man and his dog, who was more interesting in reading the *South Wales Echo* than listening to us.

I remember one gig in the Bottom Club in Cwmaman. By way of explanation, at the time in my village, we had the Top Club, which was positioned at the top of the hill, and the Bottom Club, which, not surprisingly, was at the bottom of the hill. Who said the Welsh aren't absolutely brilliant? We also had a pub in the middle, called the Middle Club. No, we're not that brilliant, it was actually called the Ivy Bush. Anyway, one night we played in the Bottom Club and it was like a morgue. Halfway through our first set, some old biddy came up and requested that we turn down the music and then another strolled over and asked us to play, 'Is This the Way to Amarillo'.

In the second half, we decided to spice it up a bit and play in our underpants. Luckily, I had always listened to my mother's advice about wearing clean underwear in case you get in an accident and need to go to hospital, or, in rock'n'roll terms, you need to go out and play the second set in your underwear just to spice it up a bit. I wish I'd thought of tucking a banana or a shuttlecock down there just to impress the girls, like the boys from Wham. But it was quite hilarious without the extra padding. All the old women were giggling while we belted out 'Looks Like Chaplin', more or less in the buff. Neither the old guy reading the paper nor his dog ever did look up.

We played in some rough old places in the Valleys, but that's what it's all about. It's the apprenticeship that all bands go through: it builds character to go out and play in front of the blue-rinse brigade, or a room full of boys looking for a scrap, or in a small bar to a handful of weird-looking fuckers out of *Deliverance*. It really taught us how to cope when things went wrong and how to deal with any situation. On the bright side, we were learning about the pleasures of smoking a little weed, and hanging out with the odd groupie or two. I thought I was already on board the rock'n'roll bus as the wheels slowly started to turn!

Before long we began to pack places out, especially the Ivy Bush and the Globe. We were turning into quite a good band with a decent following. We did some great cover songs of bands such as Pearl Jam and the Black Crowes. Not sure why, but, for whatever reason, Aberdare was mad for all that type of stuff. We started to throw in some of our own material as well, which some people thought was actually other bands' songs. A compliment, I think.

When we got more confident in our abilities, we started to spread our wings and travel to London. We would travel up, play, sleep on the floor of some mate's flat and drive back the next morning before we had to start work. It was hard labour but we loved it.

When we started to get bigger venues to play, we used to take two buses of our fans with us. It wasn't a bad deal for them. For the grand sum of about £6.50, they not only got a ticket to the best show in town, but they also enjoyed the privilege of sitting on a coach for six hours, listening to us. But everyone seemed to enjoy it. It was like a mini adventure story, 'The Welsh Let Loose in the Big Smoke', but most of the people on the bus were pissed up before we ever reached Mountain Ash.

During some of those London gigs, a couple of the boys got arrested. Nothing too serious, petty stuff, like scuffling and drunk-and-disorderly conduct, another famous trait of the Welsh nation. On one occasion, we were playing in the King's Head when our mate Jonesy – Upside-Down Head to his friends because he had a big beard and a bald head, but long strands of locks on the sides – went outside after the show to get some grub. We were packing the gear away when some guy came rushing into the club and yelled, 'Hey, boys, is that geezer with the beard with you?'

'Yeah, why?'

'He's just been knocked over by a car.'

We rushed outside and found him in the middle of the road, covered in blood and bits of kebab. We all panicked, not knowing what the hell to do. It sure would have been nice to have a book or something to refer to at that moment.

---

### A-TO-Z FOR UP-AND-COMING BANDS ON HOW TO SURVIVE THE ROCK'N'ROLL HIGHWAY

CHAPTER ONE: How to Revive a Band Member Who Smoked Too Much Dope Before Going on Stage

CHAPTER TWO: How to Say No to Minging Groupies

CHAPTER THREE: What the Hell to Do When One of Your Fans Gets Flattened by a Car While Eating a Kebab with Extra Garlic Sauce and Chilli Peppers (Light on the Salad)

---

Take it from me, someone would make a killing out of a book like that.

Anyway, we all crowded round him. He opened his eyes and muttered, 'Fucking hell, boys. That's the last time I'm coming to see you lot!'

The ambulance came and we were all stuck there until 6am, which was a pain for me because I had work in the morning. School meals don't deliver themselves, you know. But it was all worth it, just to see old Jonesy sitting up in the hospital bed in his polka-dot boxer shorts trying to pull the nurses.

While we were doing more and more gigs in London, we got a part-time agent up there called Gill Goldberg, who tried his best to get us some more high-profile bookings. Also around that time, we made a demo with a guy called Dick Crippin, who used to be in the group Ten Pole Tudor. We thought we'd made it when we travelled to Staines and slept on his floor. Surely life doesn't get much better than that?

One of the best things that happened to us at that time was meeting Steve Bush and Marshall Bird, two producers from New Zealand. We came across them after we supported Smalltown Heroes in the Borderline Club in London. They had been at the gig and had introduced themselves to Richard after the show while Kelly and I were handing out flyers promoting our next concert.

Richard, as usual, didn't raise an eyebrow when they explained to him that they were record producers and had some free time in the studio, and wondered if we wanted to be a little pet project of theirs. He didn't even mention it to us until later.

# DEMONS AND COCKTAILS

I didn't think anything of it, either, when he told us about it on the way home. To be honest, everyone claims to be a record producer in London. It's the same as when everyone says he's a major film director in Hollywood.

But we did contact them and took them up on their offer. It turned out to be one of the best moves we ever made. The demo we did with them, 'A Thousand Trees', was the actual version used to get us signed later on. Some of the other songs during the sessions we actually used on albums such as *Word Gets Around*. I liked them personally because they appreciated my style of in-your-face drumming, which gave me a lot more confidence.

When we did get signed and the label, V2 Records, wanted someone to produce the record, we agreed as a band that we owed those two guys a lot. They saw something in us that others hadn't, or had maybe chosen to ignore. We wanted to repay them and told V2 that we wanted them to produce the record for us. They agreed. Result all around.

Then we had our second major bit of luck. A promoter called Wayne Coleman was organising a series of gigs throughout South Wales under the banner of the Splash Tour. His plan was to hold events throughout the Valleys, headlined by the growing number of up-and-coming successful Welsh bands such as the Manic Street Preachers, 60 Foot Dolls, Super Furry Animals and Catatonia. They wanted local bands from each area to support them. One of the gigs was planned for the Coliseum in Aberdare, our backyard. Catatonia was the main act, supported by a band from Merthyr called the Pocket Devils. The almost legendary Pocket Devils were our main rivals in the area at the time. *Hissssss*!

## IT'S A KIND OF TRAGIC (LOVE COMPANY)

We sent him off a demo, which Wayne loved, but he told us our name was shit. He didn't hold back. 'The band's name is bloody awful,' he told me, and we couldn't get on the bill unless we changed it. Can you imagine the cheek of the fucker, telling us our name was no good? We were not amused, so we asked some other people what they thought. After listening to their feedback, we finally came to the conclusion that he was right, Tragic Love Company was a crap name. It was destined for the rubbish bin, along with all the other discarded band names over the years: Johnny and the Moondogs, the High Numbers, the Traffic.

So we met in the pub and tried to brainstorm a new name, which was much easier said than done. Our first serious attempt was Mabel Cable, after my mother. I think we thought we were Lynyrd Skynyrd, who had used the name of an old school teacher to name their band. Thankfully, we decided against it. Next came the Applejacks, which I quite liked until someone told us there was already a band of that name in the late sixties. Since the Internet wasn't available at that time to Google our picks, every time we came up with a new suggestion we had to ask the older people in the pub, no disrespect to them, if name had been taken before we got too attached.

'Shall we call ourselves the Beetles?'

'I'm sure there's already a band called that – but they had an *a* in it.'

'What about the Kinks?'

'Been done.'

'Bloody hell's bells! What about Tragically Bad Mother?'

We were getting desperate, and we had to come up with something fast. Wayne was phoning me every day because he needed to get the posters printed and the clock was ticking. The Still Born Lambs was a bizarre suggestion that sounded great after about ten pints of beer, but quite scary in the morning. I can't remember who came up with that one – probably Kelly.

Then, one afternoon, I was in my brother's bedroom and I saw a little sign on my father's old gramophone. It said 'Falcon Stereophonic'.

'That sounds good,' I thought. Falcon has such a birdie quality to it. No, I'm only joking. Stereophonic, I thought, had something about it. I waited for Kelly to come home from college on the bus to tell him the exciting news. He liked it, and our new name was official, which was really lucky because I had also written down names of several other appliances in the house that day. If it wasn't for that old radiogram system it could have been really interesting. Imagine what it would have been like the night we won the Brit Award, 'And the Best Newcomer is ... Morphy Richards.' Or a review in *NME*: '*Word Gets Around*, the great new album from Welsh rockers, the Hoovermatic Twin Tubs . . .'

With our brand-new identity we got on the bill. Our new name up in lights on Aberdare Coliseum: Catatonia, the Pocket Devils (which is an awesome name, by the way) and the Stereophonics.

The day of the gig I was a bag of nerves. It was going to be the biggest show we had played so far, and I knew there would be A&R people there. Rumour had it they had come down to see the Devils.

'What are they here to see them for? They're fucking shite!' I shouted to Kelly. 'They can't even tune their own guitars.'

## IT'S A KIND OF TRAGIC (LOVE COMPANY)

It was childish, I know, but up-and-coming bands are like that. I thought they were quite good, actually.

For the show I had cut my hair into a bob. I was trying to be like Eddie Vedder from Pearl Jam, although I probably looked more like Velma from *Scooby Doo*. Kelly had cut his hair really short and had found an old skungy, mankin' fur coat among the stage clothes at the back of the theatre and put it on for a joke before we went out.

'That looks cool as fuck,' I told him, so he wore it on stage.

Lots of people in the crowd were from Cwmaman and they knew all of our original material, which they sang along with loudly, word for word. Without sounding big-headed, we blew the Pocket Devils all the way back to bloody Merthyr. It felt great. Kelly's voice was razor-sharp.

Later, in the corridor, a man in a suit approached us. It was John Brand. He had been asked by Wayne to come along to do a seminar on getting record deals and surviving in the record industry. He had been in the business for a while with some success, and was always on the lookout for the next big thing.

He asked excitedly, 'Who wrote them songs?' We pointed at Kelly.

He looked at the singer, 'Where did you get that fur coat from? It looks brilliant!' Kelly pointed at me.

In my mind I could imagine him looking me up and down and saying, 'Fuck me, what the hell have you done with your hair?' But he didn't.

He talked to us for a while and I got the impression he was surprised that we hadn't been signed by a record company. He asked us if we would meet him the following day in Leigh

Delamare service station on the M4. So we piled into my yellow van like the Trotter family and headed East.

We weren't sure what this bloke had in mind. Earlier in our careers we'd been fucked over by some guy for the grand sum of £300, which was a small fortune to us at the time. Don't forget we were skint during those early years. Most of our money went on buying equipment or petrol to get us to gigs. It got so bad on occasion, that, when we travelled back from London after a show, we didn't have enough money to pay the Severn Bridge toll charge for a van, so went to the booth where you throw the coins in, and paid only the car rate. So I was quite suspicious of everyone, because I didn't want to get ripped off again. I listened to him talking. My first question probably mirrored my scepticism: 'How much money do you want for all this?' I was to the point and abrupt.

His reply surprised us all. 'I don't want any money.' His face was serious. 'I want to be your manager, and, when I get you a record deal, I will of course get my 20 per cent.'

'Do you think you can get us a deal?' My mood lightened up.

'I don't *think*,' he said. Our faces dropped. 'I *know* I can, and it will be in three months.'

I kicked Kelly under the table. We had found our manager. I loved his confidence; he had something special about him. I had recently read about the rise and rise of the Irish legends U2, and the massive part their manager, Paul McGuinness, had in their worldwide success. He was the fifth, and equally important, member of the biggest band on the planet. And now we had our own manager, someone who could kick down doors for us.

He told us he would telephone with some news by the end of

the week. I waited by the phone like a lovesick schoolboy. It was a long, long week. But, true to his word, he called and told us he had interest from ten companies. I put down the phone and screamed at the top of my voice. After that, things began to move really fast. I was still delivering meals to half-nourished kids in Aberdare, but now my head was buzzing with thoughts of stardom and I couldn't stop smiling. I could feel something happening; I knew something big was around the corner.

Several weeks after our initial meeting with John, we were on our way to London to meet some interested parties. We were sitting in the offices of Virgin, waiting to go in to see their top A&R person. As we waited to get summoned, John informed us that we now had every record company in the UK interested in us except Creation Records. And then, as if by magic, the phone went off. It was Creation; they also wanted to talk. He had done it: we had a full house, 37 companies all interested in us. After years of sending our demo tapes out in curry boxes, shoe boxes and any other type of gimmick we could think of to get attention, finally the music world was sitting up and taking notice. It's really strange how these things work; it's all about who you know and who that person you know knows.

We went in to see the executive at Virgin Records and, just to prove how stupid this business actually is, the woman turned out to be the one who had turned us down only six months earlier. She had come to see one of our shows in London, and didn't even wait around to talk to us after the concert. Later, she just phoned us to say that, basically, she had left early and didn't want to interrupt us, but we weren't what she was looking for. Now, a few months on, she was first in the queue of record companies ready not only to get our signature but to give us £200,000 for the pleasure. The crazy thing was that nothing had changed with us: we had the same songs, same line-up, everything.

To be honest, I didn't recognise her until Kelly noticed her name. 'I'm sure that's the same woman who turned us down,' he whispered. After she started blowing smoke up our arses, he told her that, if she looked in her bottom drawer, she would probably find one of the tapes we had sent her that she had discarded. She went red and changed the subject.

To me, most A&R people are complete dicks, couldn't spot a good band or artist if it hit them straight between the eyes. There seems to be absolutely no accountability in their roles whatsoever. How many A&Rs have been sacked down the years for passing on bands like the Rolling Stones, the Beatles or Led Zeppelin? They should be bloody fired if they fuck up, like people in proper jobs. If I was king, I would make the person who had passed on a band that later made it big under another label walk around for at least six months in a T-shirt saying something like, 'I screwed up: I turned down Oasis'. Then I would demote them to tea person.

What gets me is that they all say they're looking for the next big thing. The truth is, most of them are only looking to copy the *last* big thing. Just take Oasis, for example. I bet they were turned down by loads of companies until the guy running Creation Records took a chance and made them fucking massive. And, sure enough, next minute up sprang hundreds of carbon copies of the Manchester group, which not only sounded exactly the same but also tried to look the same. Suddenly there were hundreds of lead singers, wearing parkas, strolling about full of attitude and trying to grow their eyebrows to meet in the middle.

It's the same with the new(ish) band from Sheffield, Arctic Monkeys. Good band, probably got drawers full of rejection letters. Now that they're big, I bet the A&R people are clambering up to sign bands that sound like them and change their names to things like the Frozen Chimps or Slightly Defrosted Orang-utans. It's pathetic. I'm sure some of the A&R people really liked us when they heard our demo, but because we weren't an exact duplicate of Blur or Pulp, they wouldn't give us the time of day.

The complete turnaround in such a small space of time was really hard to take in, from not being wanted by anyone to suddenly becoming one of the UK's hottest properties. But John wasn't content with that. He was on a mission; he wanted them to come to us. He wanted the mountain to come to Mahomet. His plan was to get the A&R people camped in London to cross the Severn Bridge, parting with £2.70 of their own money in toll charges, for the privilege of seeing us. He was on a roll, and we were happy to rock'n'roll along with him.

'Don't worry: they all want to sign you. They'll come. We're in a bidding war, believe me.'

I found myself praying at night that he was right. I recall one high-powered executive from Polydor Records travelling down to the village to speak to us. He offered to take us out to a nice restaurant. Of course we all burst out laughing. 'A fucking *nice* restaurant in Cwmaman? You've more chance of seeing the Pope playing for the Glasgow Rangers!' I joked with him. I think he eventually took us down to Cardiff.

As things were heating up, John set up a major PR gig in the Filling Station in Newport. That gig was the most nerve-racking time of my life. I was glued to the bog until we went on. We did all of our own stuff and a belting version of 'I Love Rock 'N' Roll' by Joan Jett. We were on fire that night.

After the gig, John was there to meet us backstage. 'That was perfect,' he told us. 'I couldn't have asked for any more. Let's just wait for the offers to flood in.'

I thought he was mad, round the bend, and he probably was, but they did come flooding in. It was like a tidal wave coming at us and it was fucking brilliant. He had covered us in mystery, the new sensations from Wales, and now everyone wanted a piece of us.

Then we had the hard, but pleasant, part of deciding which label to go with. From the start I always wanted to go the Branson route. Everything he touched seemed to turn to gold, with maybe the exception of his ballooning stints across the Atlantic. He actually phoned us personally from his Caribbean island to try and persuade us to go with him. And, no, Kelly's mother *didn't* answer the phone that day and say, 'Yeah, if you're Richard Branson, I'm Elizabeth Taylor.' That was just a rumour, and it lasted for years.

With hindsight, I sometimes wonder if it was a good choice going with V2. I'm not sure if we would have been better off signing with a more established label. Would we have been bigger? Could we have conquered America? The V2 label at that time didn't have any clout in the States, but to be fair to Richard Branson, he did everything he could to try and get us a foothold in that tough market. On the flipside, if we had signed with one of the bigger boys, we would have just been a small fish in a really big pond and might not have achieved half of what we did. Hey, but who knows?

Anyway, we did sign with V2, and for all the right reasons. And, to be honest, they treated us like kings. We were top priority, and we were there from the start. We knew everyone in the offices by their first name; they were like family and friends.

The day we signed just showed how unstreetwise we were, proper hicks from the sticks. They took us to a posh restaurant in London. I think it was the first time I had ever drunk champagne, except for the cheap stuff they serve you at family weddings. I recall the waiter bringing us a medallion of beef, which Richard proceeded to eat in one mouthful. 'I'm starving,' he added, 'Do you do chips?'

The head waiter shook his head in disgust.

We signed that night and then proceeded to get plastered until the early hours of the morning. During the bender, we came up with a brainwave. The next morning we asked V2 for a cheque for £247,000 and a thousand pounds in cash for each of us. They must have thought we were from the cast of *The Beverly Hillbillies*. I had never seen that much money in my life, never mind put it in my back pocket. I felt like Rockefeller, or Cablefeller, or Rockacable – whoever.

We went on a spending spree in London. That sounds so rock'n'roll but, if the truth be told, we actually went fucking nuts in Topshop on Oxford Street. Imagine that, coming to London, signing a major record deal that was going to change our lives for ever, and, instead of going to the famous King's Road or Harrods, we went shopping at a high-street chain. But I didn't care. It was the first pair of Levi's I had ever bought. Up to that point I had been borrowing my brother's.

After we signed on the dotted line with V2 everything went mental. We were asked to play some gigs outside the UK. The first show was in Ireland. I had never flown before. I was 26 years old and had never been on a fucking plane; I was shitting myself. I remember when the limo taxi came and picked us up in Cwmaman. The entire village came out to wave us off. It was great, but a little bit embarrassing at the same time.

While we were in Dublin, we went to check out a competition for unsigned bands. It was called 'In the City'. Originally, we were going to be in that contest, but cancelled since we had just signed a deal. Funnily enough, Placebo actually won it. That night ended up costing us a lot of money – several years later, anyway. A girl who had taken part in the competition claimed she had given Kelly a copy of her CD and accused him of ripping off one of the songs, or part of one of her songs, and using it on our hit, 'Local Boy in the Photograph'. It was really stupid because Kelly had written the song years before he even met the girl. But she took us to court anyway. Thank God some bloke who studied medleys for a living – what a great job some people have! – concluded most of Kelly's songs and the way he sang them sounded similar to the girl's. Although the case was thrown out of court, it ended up costing us sixty grand to clear our name.

When we returned from our trip, we had calls from the BBC and HTV. They both did documentaries on us. One followed us and our girlfriends as we travelled up to Edinburgh to play at the New Year's Eve festival. We were starting to get recognised outside our own little world. Suddenly we became the public property of the whole of Wales, standing alongside the other bands that were also helping to make it an exciting place to be.

Everyone in the village was really excited for us, and our families were pleased as punch. We had lots of press and even made the front page of the *Aberdare Leader*, which was a major achievement, since it was normally reserved for updates on local criminal activities or corrupt councillors.

I remember my mother getting interviewed and telling the paper that she always knew we would do it. Of course, we had our knockers – as I mentioned earlier, it's a typical Welsh thing – but most people just wanted us to put the village on the map.

And that is what we always tried to do. We wanted to be like Tom Jones, who always brings Wales into his conversations, quickly followed by Pontypridd. Even in our first interviews, we said we were from Cwmaman, not Aberdare. Outsiders thought we were just a bunch of village bumpkins, but it was important to us. The village had given us everything: our childhoods, the swimming pools, the stories, the characters to tell the world about, the support and the encouragement.

I remember being on *Later … with Jools Holland* after our second album, *Performance and Cocktails*, had hit the charts and Jools was struggling to pronounce Cwmaman.

'Can't I just say Aberdare?' he pleaded.

'No. We're from Cwmaman.'

He looked at the camera and said, 'Ladies and gentlemen, all the way from Cwmamnmomonnn – the Stereophonics.'

'I remember the Stereophonics – or Tragic Love Company, as they were – playing in a field by a pub just outside Aberdare to about ten people sitting on a giant tartan blanket. Meanwhile, in London, bands were getting signed because they drank in the right pub, or had the right hair. The Stereophonics deserved to get to where they got because they worked hard and paid their dues. No one can ever take that away from them.

'I'd be lying if I ever said I was a fan. Being a Merthyr boy, I loved soul and dance music too much, but I always admired the fact that they wore their Valleys roots on their sleeve. That in itself told kids that they weren't the rubbish that the Tory government had been telling us South Wales was for twenty years.

'Stuart, I've got to know personally and he's a star. A big heart and personality, he's a natural whether drumming, presenting or on his radio show. Enormously likable, he's become one of those people Wales needs just to give us an idea of who we are. Okay, we'll forgive him some of his musical tastes and his hair, but then again he's an Aberdare boy. And that's why we love him so dearly.'

**Jon Owen, actor, TV presenter and the one and only singer with rival band, the Pocket Devils**

# CHAPTER 4

# WORD GETS ALOUD

After years of slogging it up and down the M4, struggling to get ourselves heard, finally we had our feet on the first rung of the ladder. It all happened so fast. Within about six weeks we had met John Brand, gone into Battery Studios and done another demo with Bird and Bush, and secured a record deal with Richard Branson's new label. I had to pinch myself to make sure I hadn't died and gone to Penarth.

Getting signed with V2 was a great start and it separated us from the tens of thousands of other bands still trying to get noticed, but we knew there was a lot of hard work in front of us, that we had to get out there and get our stuff full on into people's faces. We recognised that we had to be the best at writing songs and playing live. We needed to build on the popularity of the band far beyond the handful of loyal mates and fans from our home town, but we took it a rung at a time. Sometimes it felt as if we took two steps up and three steps back. And, just when we thought we had finally reached the top of the ladder, someone would sneak up and pull it from beneath our feet.

It's funny because there were those who thought we had become instant millionaires as soon as we signed on the dotted line, as if we were lucky, jammy lottery-jackpot-winning bastards. They actually believed we would be headlining at venues such as the Reading Festival and driving round in stretch limousines, drinking pink champagne the day after we signed. I wish it were that easy, but unfortunately the record industry doesn't work like that. They still want their pound of flesh just like any other business. We did get on the bill of the V97 Festival, but we were bottom of the list. The only one below us was the bloke who cleaned up the rubbish when it was all over. But, hey, we were out of the sackful of chaff and into the wheat pile at least.

We spent some of our new fortune on a much better tour bus. It was a Mercedes. It was great: it had a video player, a toilet that actually worked, and a table we could play cards on or roll anything up we may need to. It was the dog's bollocks. Sadly, my old yellow post-office van was unceremoniously sold off to the highest bidder for 50 quid.

Although the way we travelled was a lot more comfortable and we didn't have to take turns lying in the back with the equipment as before, we had to travel much greater distances now. Our agent, Scott Thomas, got us one of those tours that are well known in the business as 'toilet tours', which means we played in every shithole in the country. On top of that, the sequencing of venues didn't seem to have any rhyme or reason. It was as if someone had just thrown darts at a map of the UK, and whatever order they stuck was the order of where we played.

But at that point we were grateful to play everywhere and anywhere we could, so we didn't complain too much. We would play in a small-town venue and do it again six months later, this time hopefully with an extra sixty or seventy new fans there to see us. It was our masterplan until the singles and album hit the shops.

Being on the road constantly, travelling up and down the country with all the late nights, eventually took its toll on me. It seemed like I was ill all of the time. Any viruses or bugs that happened to be floating about would find me and cling on for dear life. Okay, maybe it wasn't just the travelling. I'm sure the hard partying and the physical exertion of drumming night after night may have helped a little. Maybe it was the fact that I ignored Newton's simple theory of motion that says, 'Drummer who is life and soul of party and always in constant motion needs to slow down and get some rest or pretty soon he will be run himself dry.' And that's what I did: run dry.

But I wasn't the only one feeling the strain. One night we played at the Leadmill, in Sheffield. It was one o'clock in the morning and there was no one there, no one at all, not a bloody soul. We weren't sure if we should go out and play or just pack up our gear and move on. But eventually a couple of vampires turned up and we went out and gave it our all. By the time we did pack up and get on the road, it was already the early hours of a cold morning and we still had to get down to Brighton to kick off the Essential Festival at midday. Nicola, my girlfriend at the time, was with me and we drove down together in her car. I got about three hours of sleep before we had to go on stage. I was knackered; we all were.

During our second song, Kelly's voice packed up altogether. The pressure of all the touring had claimed another victim. He stopped mid-song, threw off his guitar and walked slowly off-stage. I didn't know what was going on; I thought he'd left something on the side of the stage, or maybe just remembered he'd left the bath running. After a few minutes, I realised he wasn't coming back. I looked at Richard, he looked at me. I wasn't sure what the hell we were going to do because neither of us could sing for toffee. Until that moment I never appreciated how much we relied on Kelly's voice. Losing it wasn't like snapping a bass string or ripping a drum skin; we didn't have a spare voice in the bag.

So Richard and I finished the rest of the song and trooped off to lots of boos and catcalls. I remember the review in one of the papers the next day. It will stay with me until the day I'll die. It simply said, 'The Stereophonics – the most unessential start to the Essential Festival.' Absolutely brilliant! What a clever, witty bastard who wrote that!

Driving home that night we were all feeling low and knew it was time for a rest, including our agent and the record company personnel, who had been pushing us really hard, so we took a few weeks off to recuperate.

But it wasn't all doom and gloom. We did a couple of big support gigs: Skunk Anansie, the Manics and then right out of the blue, we were asked to support the one and only Who at Earl's Court in London for two nights.

'The Who?' I recall yelling out when Kelly told me. 'You mean *the* Who, the Who as in "My Generation", *Tommy* and all that stuff?'

## WORD GETS ALOUD

I love the Who. I still watch *The Kids are Alright* whenever I'm at home and drunk; I must have seen that rockumentary a thousand times. Even today when I'm entertaining and get drunk I normally put it on, followed by the *AC/DC – Live at Donington* DVD and, if everyone is still awake, *The Tragically Hip: That Night in Toronto* DVD. I know people take the piss – 'Oh, Stuart must be drunk – the Who DVD is out of the case' – but I don't care.

I couldn't believe it when we turned up at the Earl's Court gig. Seventeen thousand rock fans waiting to squeeze into the great arena. I remember looking around and shitting myself, amazed at just how big it was. We met Roger Daltrey first. He later became a big fan of the band; he loved Kelly's voice. He's a top guy and was one of the main reasons I got the gig in Swansea Liberty Stadium in 2007 supporting the Who with my new band, Killing for Company. But I'll come to that later.

It was a great experience for us at the time and, as the MasterCard advert might say: 'Fender American Vintage '62 Jaguar electric guitar in metallic ice-blue: £750; a pair of trusty Ray-Ban sunglasses and a tight leather vintage jacket to look rock-star cool: £350. Opening for the legendary Who: priceless'.

The strange, and rather sad thing I recall about that gig was seeing each member of the Who arrive in a separate limo and go to his separate dressing room. As far as I could tell they didn't communicate with each other at all, other than when they were actually on stage performing. After the encore they left in separate cars. I remember hoping we never ended up that way. Not us, not the Stereophonics – we would always be friends for ever and ever. 'We are the three fucking musketeers,' I told myself, and crossed my fingers.

Our singles were also released during that time. The first couple were never going to be smash hits, but they did make a small dent in the charts and it was still a great feeling to hear them played on the radio. I remember singing at the top of my voice in the car to 'Local Boy' the first time I heard it. I wanted to stop my car and get on the roof and cry out, 'That's me and my bloody mates playing that! Ain't it good?' But it was such a massive struggle to get our songs on the radio at all. Back then, there wasn't a real alternative radio station to compete with Radio 1; they were the be-all and end-all, the Brazil football team of the airwaves. There was no XFM or Virgin. There was Radio 2, but at the time it was classed as an old men's station, playing tracks from has-beens and safe presenters who were all biding their time to DJ heaven. So, if we were going to make it, we had to get onto Britain's top station. And, in my opinion, we deserved the airplay. We had some great singles from that first LP: 'Local Boy', 'Traffic', 'Thousand Trees'.

Our record company and our management had to work really hard to get us any airtime at all. We released 4 singles from the first album and, although the BBC said they would support us, when push came to shove they always went with someone else. They gave John a 100 per cent guarantee that they would support us and play 'Traffic', but they never did. That was one of the main reasons we ended up releasing 'The Bartender and the Thief' as the first single from the second album. I think we just thought, 'What the hell! They ain't going to play it anyway, so let's enjoy ourselves.'

We had little, if any, real meaningful airplay for the first album. But we didn't let it get us down too much because, out of the blue, we were nominated for a Brit Award for Best Newcomer in 1998. I remember going on *The Big Breakfast Show* a day or so before the event with Denise van Outen and Johnny Vaughan. They had the Brit Award on the table. Denise asked if we thought we had a chance of winning it.

'No,' I replied. And I didn't say that because I was being all cocky or modest. Deep down, I didn't really think we even had a chance; I was just happy to be going. I had watched it on TV for years and now I had a chance to enjoy it live.

We were up against Travis, Embrace, Shola Ama, Finley Quaye and the main favourites, the all-girl group, All Saints. Luckily for us, it was down to the public to vote for the winner. Up to the last weekend before the ceremony, we were behind All Saints, but then, for reasons known only to our manager John, that weekend we pissed on them. Not in the physical sense, but we overtook them by around 5,000 votes. I'm still not sure what kind of wheeling and dealing went on behind the scenes, but whatever John had done, it was a fantastic job. I'm not saying it was all down to the hand of John Brand, but I know he helped push it in our direction by getting our growing fan base to vote.

He told me later that he knew we had won by Sunday, but decided not to tell us; he wanted to see our faces. Apparently everyone else from the record company knew we had won it as well. Come the night of the awards, I sat there half-cut, kitted out in my favourite Topshop gear, feeling the height of trendy. It was one of the biggest thrills of my life when our name was finally called out. The women with us from V2 were crying and the men were grinning at their rivals like the cat that got the cream. At the time I was too naïve to understand that it was also a big deal for the label as well. Most of the team at V2 had left high-paying jobs at other recording companies, just for the chance to work with Branson and produce great bands. The award was as much for all the effort, time and love they had put into us as it was for the writing and playing of the songs that we had done. We were part of a big team, and Richard, Kelly and I were just the tip of the V2 iceberg.

After that, we never won another Brit. We were nominated a few times in the following years and I definitely feel we should have won one for Best Album in 2000 with *Performance and Cocktails*, but it went to the very popular Scottish band, Travis. Even though I think they are a great bunch of guys, very genuine and down-to-earth, I just think the year they won Best Band and Best Album was slightly unfair. It would be wrong of me to say we should have won Best Band, because that's very subjective, but I think we should have at least taken the Best Album award. To me it was much better than Travis's *The Man Who*. The songs were better and fuller and it was much better produced. But we didn't win, and that's just the way it goes. Sometimes the best teams don't win the FA Cup either, but my one Brit Award still sits proudly on the mantelpiece in my house. I may not have as many as Robbie or Noel but I try to remind myself that it's one more than most people have.

The media had a field day reporting our supposed rivalry with Travis. To set the record straight once and for all, I may have told Kelly when I first saw them in their early days that they would never get anywhere, but that was just a competitive thing. I think they write some great tunes and I love meeting up with them; they are top guys.

My crap prediction about Travis wasn't half as bad as Kelly's prediction for Coldplay. He once said that they were 'utter shite' and would 'never last'. To be fair to him, I think he got at least part of his statement right, for a change: I think they are utter shite. But Coldplay did last, and they are undoubtedly one of the biggest bands in the world. For what it's worth, I still think they are nothing more than a poor man's U2 with a vegetable-rights-for-all, bracelet-wearing singer, who looks clean-cut even when he tries to be scruffy. Maybe they should have been called Cleancut.

After the Brits, we went out on the road again, but now our shows got much more support. More people had heard of us and wanted to find out what all the fuss was about.

Unfortunately, I still hadn't learnt how to tour and take care of myself and I fell ill yet again. I was at home in bed when the news filtered through that our first album had hit the UK charts, straight in at Number 6. Apparently, I missed the mother of all piss-ups too. The boys phoned me from Germany. I couldn't believe it: I knew most of my family and friends were going to buy it, but even if they had bought a couple of thousand copies each, there still had to have been thousands of others who had gone out of their way to get it. I remember the feeling when I got the music papers and saw our album in print in the charts. The album with all the songs we had written in our bedroom or at the club, there among all the big shots like Oasis, Radiohead, Texas, the Prodigy. It was unbelievable. If I hadn't been on medication, I would have gone to the pub and got plastered myself.

As soon as I got better and went out on tour again, I went straight back to my partying ways. This time I became seriously ill and was rushed to hospital. It took them a while even to figure out what was wrong with me. At one stage I thought they were going to give up and bring in some witch doctor to cover me in herbs and leeches, but instead they put me in an infectious-diseases ward.

They finally diagnosed me with glandular fever combined with pneumonia. Trust me to come down with not one but two major ailments at the same time. The doctor told me my partying days had to stop for a while.

'How long, Doc?'

'About six months at the minimum.'

'Six fucking months? You're telling me I can't drink for six months? I play in a band. I'm the drummer. The *drummer*! Partying is what rock drummers are supposed to do.' I could imagine Keith Moon turning in his grave.

When I did get out, I think I lasted three weeks. To make matters worse, we were at the time scheduled to go to the States for the first time ever to play a concert and make a video. So, while the boys and John flew first-class to the United States of America, I sat in a hospital bed with a bottle of warm Lucozade and a bunch of grapes, surrounded by a ward full of people who looked like the cast from *Shaun of the Dead*.

When they phoned me, I could hear the sirens of New York cop cars in the background. It reminded me of *Starsky and Hutch*. I was so envious and pissed off. The gig we were supposed to play was cancelled, so they did some sightseeing, some radio interviews and some heavy drinking before they flew to LA to make the video for 'Traffic'. It was a bad time for me. I was determined to recover and get back on the road as soon as possible.

Back in the village, our TV appearances were causing a major stir. Everyone came out to watch us en masse in the pub whenever we appeared on *Top of the Pops*, or *CD:UK* with Ant and Dec and Cat Deeley. I remember appearing the first time on the legendary BBC show; it was a big deal for me. *Top of the Pops*, man! I remember growing up and watching it religiously every week. At Christmas time I would sit in front of my TV and try to record songs on a crappy little handheld recorder while my mother was busy doing the dinner. Everyone who was anyone wanted to play *Top of the Pops*.

When we first got to the famous studio, I remember the shivers dancing up my spine. 'Fucking hell! *Top of the* fucking *Pops*!' I could feel the history in the building slapping me across the face. I walked onto the stage where Marc Bolan and AC/DC and many others had played – sorry, mimed – down the years. And who could forget the one and only introduction music by Led Zeppelin? They had all performed within these four walls and now we were about to join them; it was all too much to take in.

I remember going home after they had recorded the episode, and being met with the same Welsh Valleys pride that was often waiting with bated breath for our return. I would stroll into the Ivy Bush thinking I was Elvis Presley.

'Hi, Stu, saw you on *Top of the Pops* last night. You're an ugly bastard!'

'The BBC should have put a warning on before they showed your ugly face, or at least put a bag on your head!'

The room would be in uproar. I was often the butt of their jokes, and I loved every minute of it.

I remember that on one occasion we were recording 5 songs for *Top of the Pops* while Oasis were on the other stages doing the same. We both had heavy touring schedules, so someone decided to tape the songs in one go. It was really weird. We would do a song, go off and change while they did a song. I remember Liam Gallagher in his black shades, the height of coolness, shouting across between takes, 'Hey Stuey, how's it going, top man?' I remember every detail, including all the other people in the room turning to stare at me in amazement, and me with the smuggest grin I could possibly muster on my puss.

Another funny story was the time that we were playing on *Top of the Pops* and Robbie Williams was also performing. I think it was when he was rebuilding his career after getting the boot from Take That, and was performing one of his early singles. After the show, we were all in the BBC club having a few beers. Robbie latched onto me and we talked about golf and exchanged numbers. He asked if I wanted to go to a club with him later that night. Unfortunately, I needed to get home to Nicola, whom I was now living with. And it was obvious to me that the boy from Stoke was not just high on life, and at the time I didn't do drugs. So I declined. When I got home, Nicola told me that some idiot had phoned about three in the morning and claimed to be Robbie Williams. She told him to fuck off and slammed the phone down; she was gutted when she found out it was really him.

We tried to be true to our word about putting Cwmaman on the world map, and we did a video for 'Traffic' in the street that

Kelly and I were brought up in, which was aired on *Top of the Pops*. I remember the piss-up in the Ivy Bush later that night.

I always loved doing the *Top of the Pops* show. It's a bloody shame it's gone; we shouldn't have allowed it. It was our national institution, a bit like the royal family, Stonehenge or rainy bank holidays. We shouldn't have let it go without a huge fight.

Things were moving fast for us, and it was hard to appreciate. We still lived in the village up until the release of our second album. Richard was the first to go. He split with his girlfriend and moved up to London after a strong rumour surfaced that a top fashion model had commented in a magazine that she thought the bass guitarist from our band was gorgeous. Next, thing he just ups sticks and leaves, like Dick Whittington without the cat. Just his guitar strapped across his back and a couple of quid in his arse pocket. Next, Kelly followed more or less the same path. He split with Emma and moved for the glamour of the bright city lights.

But London wasn't for me. I had something more serious to do, like ask Nicola to marry me. I remember the occasion vividly. It was very romantic. I got down on one knee, clutching an expensive engagement ring in my teeth. The whole restaurant along the river bank was quiet. The violinist I had hired was waiting for the right moment for her to say yes before he lit up the room with his music.

Okay, you know that's a bunch of crap, so here's the truth. I actually asked her while her mother was out shopping and we were lying in bed at her home.

'Come on, let's get married,' I said, trying to look all sexy and suave. I was a full-on love tiger. Luckily, she accepted.

# DEMONS AND COCKTAILS

We got hitched in Court Coleman in Bridgend. It's an old manor-style house, extremely classy. Kelly and Richard volunteered to play a few songs for us during the day. They did an acoustic set, which was really good of Kelly since I had also employed him to stand on top of the wedding cake next to a plastic bride for most of the celebration.

At the time, Nicola was working as an occupational therapist in Bridgend. We moved into a house in Park View in Cwmaman. It was small and compact, but a practical, terraced house on the same street as Richard's mother and father. We lived there for a few years until I made a shed full of money from the gigging and the records, and then, after some soul searching, and nagging from Nicola, we bought a house in another part of Aberdare called Abernant. It was once owned by the wealthy Williams family, who made their fortune supplying coal in the area. We viewed it on a bright summer's day, which was unusual weather for the Valleys. But, to be honest, it wouldn't have mattered if we had seen it on the worst day of the year.

It was brilliant. You couldn't hear a sound: no cars, no people staggering home drunk or shouting in the street. All you could hear were the birds and the silence. It had five bedrooms, its own grounds and a large wall surrounding the place. When I was growing up, I used to pass the posh houses in Abernant and wonder what it would be like to live there. Then there I was, chopsey Cable, the class clown, living with the rest of the well-off people. I even had an electric gate. Fucking hell, the only people from Cwmaman that were greeted by electric gates were prisoners and the wives of prisoners! I spent a small fortune doing it up, but it was well worth it. In fact, my wife and son still live there today.

Initially, my mother acted as though she wasn't impressed with it. I don't think she would have been impressed if I had bought Buckingham Palace and painted it pink and attached a big curly wig to one of the towers. But later in life she told me she couldn't believe one of her sons was living in one of the posh houses in the town. I remember my cousin from Liverpool coming down to visit us. We were still in the middle of moving at the time. He thought I was a super-rich rock star, like Keith Richards' type of rich. His faced dropped when we met him at our house on Park Street. I could sense his disappointment.

But that changed when I took him to my new pad, which was getting some work done on it. He stopped in his tracks. 'Now this is what I call a proper rock star's house,' he muttered.

Things were going great for me and the band. Our first big gig was scheduled for Cardiff Castle. The concert was originally set to be a small affair during the European Summit, which was on in Cardiff that same weekend. We had just gone into Real World studios to record our second album, *Performance and Cocktails*, with the legendary Peter Gabriel, when John Brand came to tell us that the show had gone from a manageable 2,000 people to 10,000. It seemed that everyone wanted to see the boys from the Valleys. He said we needed to come up with something better than 'The Stereophonics play Cardiff Castle'. It sounded too boring, too predictable. He wanted something people would remember.

We were all racking our brains, when Richard piped up, 'Let's call it "Cwmaman Feel the Noise".' It was a play on the old Slade song, 'Cum On Feel the Noize'. I was shocked. I think everyone in the room was taken aback. Richard hadn't said a word in fifteen years – well, anything of great significance, anyway – and then he comes out with a gem like that.

'Who the hell plugged him in?' I thought to myself. 'Where did you get that from?' I asked him.

Then, in a typical Richard way, he shrugged his shoulders, smirked and went back to plucking his guitar. So that was that: 'Cwmaman Feel the Noise' was the flag we would march behind for our biggest concert to date.

The gig in the Castle became big news all over the principality. They hadn't had a concert there for many years. Not since the seventies, when bands such as the Rolling Stones, Status Quo and Queen, supported by Thin Lizzy, had performed there. We were in grand company. All the tickets sold out in a few weeks. I couldn't believe what was going on. I had phone calls from people looking for tickets. We had interviews with the BBC and HTV, and all the music press and local newspapers. Finally, we were riding the wave of the new Welsh music scene. An oxymoron only a few short years before, 'Welsh' and 'music', that is. Now it was different. We had waited for years for a top Welsh band to emerge, and now there were four or five at the same time, and we were among them.

On that night, we wanted everything to be perfect. We tried to make the stage look like the Top Club in Cwmaman. We had silver strips hanging down, as in an old workers' club. I'm not sure if people understood that at the time, or just thought we were poor and that was all we could afford. I recall standing there during the sound check and looking out at the grass areas. It was intimidating.

'What if no one turns up? What if they don't like us? What if aliens land and take Kelly hostage? Who's going to sing?' My head was racing with mad, stupid thoughts. We were staying opposite in the Angel Hotel. I must have spent the entire afternoon on the toilet. Our dressing room in the Castle was miles away from the stage, and I nearly crapped myself when I heard the noise rising up from the crowd when they realised we were coming on. I had never heard anything like it before. I was shaking in my boots, my hair was standing on end. And you imagine my hair standing on end – it can almost touch the full moon!

The sound was deafening. It took me a couple of songs to appreciate fully where we were and what the hell I was doing there. The lights came on after our third or fourth song, and I looked out to see all these people staring back at me. What a weird but fantastic feeling! That was the first time I felt like a proper rock star. There was nothing fake about this.

Everyone I knew from the village was there. I think it was Kelly who said to one newspaper that, if anyone was looking to burglarise a few houses that night, they should go to Cwmaman. He was right. The entire village were out front singing their socks off. Even today they still tell the stories about people walking around pissed and getting arrested. Richard Jones, *the* Richard Jones who had left the band, apparently found his old man on a student campus a few miles away, bollock naked. The police had him in the back of the van. That was all that was ever disclosed about what happened. Some things should really be kept hush-hush.

One of the most bizarre and best things of the night was John telling us to get straight into the waiting cars when we came off stage. The police were going to block off the main road off for the crowds to leave the Castle, and if we didn't get right to the cars, we would be caught up in the mad rush.

So, as soon as we played the last note of our encore and Kelly had thanked everyone for coming, we raced off the stage. There were security guards waiting on the stairs. They wrapped us in towels and had torches to direct the way. We raced to the cars, piled in and they shot away. We were whisked away, all of 500 yards to the hotel. Hilariously, the car I was in with Nicola went the wrong way and we ended up in a dead-end street. We had to reverse back out.

Now how fucking rock'n'roll is that? Only a couple of months earlier we would finish our gig, pose for a few photographs and then just dismantle our equipment and drive home ourselves.

Later, in my hotel room with Nicola, I was lying on the bed and sweating. 'How do you feel?' she asked.

'How fucking nuts was that?' I couldn't put into words how I really felt. I had a quick shower, and when I came out, Nicola told me to have a look out the window.

I opened it and remember seeing streams and streams of people leaving the Castle, singing our songs and dancing about. Some were kissing and hugging. I couldn't believe they had all come to see us and, what was more, they really looked as if they had enjoyed themselves. I just sat there opened-mouthed. Then someone saw me and shouted up, 'It's Stuart!'

About five thousand people looked up at me.

'Jump,' someone shouted. 'We'll catch you.'

To be honest, the way I felt, I would have – I was on such a high I felt as if I could fly.

I dressed as quickly as I could and headed to the bar. It was party time. There was an impressive guest list, too, including the Manics, Catatonia, Super Furry Animals and some of the cast from the brilliant film *Twin Town*. I half expected, and hoped, that old Shakin' Stephens would be there. I could have done with a mass chorus of 'Green Door'. Unfortunately, he wasn't.

I sat with James Dean Bradfield from the Manics. After a few ales he turned and said to me, 'I'm jealous as fuck of what you did tonight.'

I was shocked. 'What do you mean?'

'I'm jealous you did the Castle.'

'But you guys could have done it a long time before us.' I honestly believed that. They were on their third or fourth album; we hadn't even done our second yet.

He shook his head. 'No, we don't have the Welsh people like you guys. You've really got them. You did it on home soil.'

I let his words sink in. Looking back now, I think he was right. In my opinion, the Welsh people could relate better to Kelly's lyrics and his way of telling little stories, maybe slightly better than they could with some of the Manics' classic hits such as 'Motorcycle Emptiness' and 'From Despair to Where'. On the other hand, they had much more of an advantage with the people outside Wales. The non-Welsh took them on board more readily than they did us. Many tagged us with just being a good band for Welsh people, which I strongly disagreed with.

Fair play to James: it was big of him to say that. Especially with the bit of bad blood we had between us, which had started when we supported them at a gig in Manchester a few months earlier. At the show all the electrics went off in the middle of our set –

the lights, the PA, the amps, everything. I recall someone from the crowd shouting out in a thick Welsh accent, 'Hey Butt, has anyone got ten bob for the meter?' Our driver and photographer extraordinaire, Julian, had been backstage and was adamant that the Manics had pulled the plug because we were playing so well and would have blown them off the stage.

I still don't think it's true. No, I *know* it's not true. I have got to know the members of the group since that incident, and they are real, honest, talented guys. At that time they would have been much too good for any support band to upstage anyway. But James and the Manics' Nicky Wire weren't happy with the accusations and were still hanging onto some bad feelings.

The rest of the night in the Angel Hotel was party, party, party time. I can't remember much else that what went on. I got to bed about 6am, a huge smile on my face. The next day, even though I had a super-bad head, I felt one hundred feet tall. The reviews in the *Western Mail*, the main newspaper of Wales, the next day were extremely complimentary. I wanted to walk around all day with a big sign on my back saying, I'M STUART CABLE, DRUMMING WITH THE 'PHONICS. But we still had an album to finish. We headed off back to Bath to the studio. Can you imagine that? One minute playing in front of 10,000 screaming fans, the next alone in a soundproofed booth, headphones on, adding some finishing touches to 'Plastic California', while in the next studio, Black Grape were there playing like fuck and eating dope as if it were fairy cakes. It's a dirty job, but someone's got to do it.

'Drummer, musician, broadcaster, television personality, Welshman, and all-round nice guy. Stuart's charm, genuine warmth and unique voice have made him a true son of Wales.'

**John Brand, ex-manager, Stereophonics**

## CHAPTER 5

# PERFORMANCE AND JACKBOOTS

I had a sneaky feeling our second album was going to be good, but even I didn't realise just how much it would change our lives for ever, in terms of both fame and wealth. I had always been very confident in the ability of the band, and when Kelly turned up with a stack of songs already written and raring to go, I couldn't wait to get our teeth into them.

Whatever people said about Kelly, he was very prolific when it came to knocking out hits. To me, he was the Ben Elton of songwriting. He always reminded me of a professional snooker player because, while Rich and I were still glowing at the success of our first album and the Cardiff Castle gig, Kelly was already thinking a few shots ahead, totally focused on taking us to the next level.

As I mentioned earlier, we found it hard to get the airplay we deserved with the first batch of singles from our debut album. That was one of the main reasons we picked 'The Bartender and the Thief' as the debut single from the new one. Then a small miracle happened. Six weeks before the actual release date of the single, the BBC heard it, and not only liked it but put it straight up there on the 'A' list. It was really tough to get on the 'A' list, especially with Radio 1, because they played all the new fad music of the moment, all the dance stuff. I think the fact that the video was brilliant and was constantly being played on MTV helped sway their decision as well.

Anyway, we were suddenly on Radio 1's 'A' list, which, if my memory serves me right, meant it would get played something like 45 times per week and that it would be played to the morning and evening drive-time markets. What a difference a song makes! I think we had more plays of 'Bartender' in one week than all of our other songs put together. After years of hard work, success finally hit us overnight; it moved us to the top of the rock'n'roll ladder. We were up there with the big boys. We went from playing small venues of around 500 people, and that was on a good night, to suddenly playing gigs for 2,000-plus fans at some of the biggest venues across the country, such as the NEC near Birmingham and the arenas in Sheffield, Newcastle and Scotland.

After the full release of the *Performance and Cocktails* album, everything went mental for us. We followed up 'Bartender' with a host of hits such as 'Pick a Part That's New', 'Hurry Up and Wait', 'Just Looking' and 'I Wouldn't Believe Your Radio'. Life was sweet and the money we started to earn was sweeter still.

I remember that, during the original recording session of the album, a heated disagreement broke out in the studio between the band and our new A&R man, Dave Wibberly. He had come down to check out the new material. Dave had joined us after we were signed and he really didn't know what made us tick. None of us had ever been followers of fashion or trends – you only have to look at my clothes to see that. But, as far as music was concerned, if we liked it and it appealed to us, we liked it; if we didn't, we didn't. It was as simple as that. We refused to change our style to what everyone else was doing.

In the music scene at the time, lots of bands were putting horn sections into their songs. The Manics did it. So did Dodgy and Kula Shaker, and even Oasis. Everyone was doing it. It became the new craze, the 'in' thing to do.

It seemed to us that David had turned up with only one thing on his mind, and that was to get us to jump on the bandwagon. We sat there on the large settee, drinking tea and listening to the playbacks from the mixing desks. I remember he spoke with a uvular 'r', a bit like Jonathan 'Woss'. He muttered, 'Good, good,' but then he left a pause. 'But I fink a few of the twacks should have some horns on them.' He started to reel off some shit or other about how successful this song or that song had been.

Kelly looked at me, I looked at Kelly. I felt like saying, 'Oh, mate, we'll put horns on any song you want as long as you stand on the chair and shout, "Release Rudolf the red-nosed reindeer", you stupid talentless twat!' I was bubbling inside. We were working hard, most days for 20 hours, just for this guy to turn up and give us the old 'Yes, yes – *but* …' I always hated people who did that: 'Hi, I like it, *but* …'; 'I think it would be a good single, *but* …'

Kelly handled the situation forcefully but a little more diplomatically than I expected him to. 'I thought that would be your reaction,' he said.

'What do you mean?' Dave replied.

'Have you got anything to add other than we should try to make it sound like every other band around at the moment?' He added, 'This is just typical A&R bullshit.'

Dave was taken aback, but Kelly wasn't finished. 'Just because everyone else is doing it, it doesn't mean *we* have to.' To be fair to Kelly, he knew exactly what he wanted from a song long before it ever came alive in the studio. His tunes and the stories seemed to play out in his mind like little mini film scripts.

I chipped in, 'Dave, I'm not sure if you should be A&R-ing for us. Obviously you aren't on the same wavelength as us at all.'

He went quiet and didn't say much for the rest of the day. Not surprisingly, he didn't last long after that. I think we were the only band in the history of the music business to sack their A&R man. We told the head of the record company we didn't want to work with him. Again, I'm not slagging him off. He was quite a nice guy *but* … what he knew about music you could write on the back of a postage stamp.

It makes me wonder sometimes how some of the A&R people get their jobs in the first place. To me, he couldn't see the wood for the thousand trees, and rather than just going with it and being part of our team, he thought he had to have his input. I don't think he could have faulted the album as it stood. It was tight, the songs were great and it had a good balance to it. But that's just what it's like in this business. What I've noticed in my short time in the rock world is that there are some people in this industry who just like to turn around at posh dinner parties and say, 'Oh yes, that was my idea. I was the one who told the group to do that, and yes, of course, I told them they should wear knitted cardigans and white socks.' It is all bollocks and still makes me mad.

Nevertheless, during the making of the album, Kelly and I were still the best of mates. You couldn't split us with a razorblade. One night, he pulled me down to the studio at around two in the morning. He sat in front of the piano and started playing. I didn't realise he could actually play the thing. Apparently, he had learnt just four chords only a few weeks before. 'Stu, I've written this thing. Have a listen.' He then played 'I Stopped to Fill My Car Up'.

When it was finished he nervously asked me what I thought.

I think I just said, 'Fucking hell, Kel! We've *got* to record that on the album tomorrow. It's brilliant.' He was chuffed. We had a few cans and went off to bed. I was excited.

The next morning, we told everyone about the new song and our thoughts about including it on the album. After they listened to it, they all agreed. I know the song is based on an old shaggy-dog story, one of those urban myths about a bank robber turned killer getting into the back of a car while some innocent person stops to put petrol in it. It was one of those tales you hear around the camp fire that makes you snuggle into your sleeping bag and look about at the darkened trees, praying for morning to appear; people swear it's true because it once happened to a friend of a friend's uncle's cousin's mate who lived near the chip shop. You know what I mean! But it was great.

And I think Kelly was brave to attempt it. It could have easily been a flop, but it worked so well. He had turned it into a classic, spooky tune with a haunting lyric, and the way he delivered the vocals was spine-chilling. We added some weird drum shit to it to ensure the atmosphere travelled through the song. I was actually playing with wooden brushes to give it the effect. I loved playing it live, and it is still one of my favourite tunes that I have ever done with the band.

I think the videos we recorded to go along with the second album were another big reason why it was so successful. We worked with a great director, Pinko, who was full of enthusiasm and ideas. The main concept of most of the videos was based on certain classic films. The one for 'Pick a Part' was a copy of *The Italian Job*, and we shot it in Turin, where they actually made the original film. 'I Wouldn't Believe Your Radio' was shot in Granada, Spain, where they filmed all the spaghetti Westerns. 'Hurry Up and Wait' was a rip-off of the old *M*A*S*H* episodes and we filmed it in Australia, just outside Sydney, while we were out there touring.

The two videos I really remember most were for 'The Bartender and the Thief' and 'Just Looking'. For 'Bartender' we were in Thailand and we stopped over in Bangkok before the shoot. Once there, we headed straight to the seediest part of town. I remember walking down the main street and going into this place we called the Kiss bar, because it had the same logo as the band Kiss. We walked in and there was a big bar in the centre with all these beautiful creatures dancing on top of it with hardly any clothes on. To make it even more enjoyable, AC/DC was on the jukebox.

John had given us a warning about the place. He told us to watch out for ourselves and not to get sucked into the obvious attractions on parade. Let me tell you, that's a lot easier said than done! It was a really erotic environment and full of temptation, especially for three boys from a small village, who were more used

*Above left*: My mother looking gorgeous.

*Above right*: First picture of me with my old man.

*Below*: Playing soccer for the village team. I'm the good looking one at the back, second from the left.

# Blaengwawr Comprehensive School

NAME _Stuart Cable_  FORM _5K_  TERM _Easter_

SESSIONS ABSENT _14_  SESSIONS LATE _0_  AGE _16_  NO. IN FORM _22_  NEXT TERM STARTS _1st Sept_

| SUBJECT | MARK or GRADE | TERM'S WORK | GENERAL REMARKS | INIT |
|---|---|---|---|---|
| English Language | 45 | C | Good. Stuart is making an effort with his work but some of his answers would benefit from a bit more careful thought. | AJ. |
| English Literature | | | | |
| Drama | | | | |
| Mathematics - numeracy | 88 | A | Excellent. | PB |
| History | 51 | C | Good. But Stuart can still improve on this. | Cm |
| Geography | 31% | D† | Stuart has no chance of passing unless he revises more thoroughly and sorts himself out. | |
| Geology | | | | |
| Scripture | | | | |
| Welsh | | | | |
| French | | | | |
| Latin/German | | | | |
| Music | | | | |
| Physics | | | | |
| Chemistry | | | | |
| Biology | | | | |
| General Science | | | | |
| Rural Science | | | | |
| Social Studies | | | | |
| Art/Pottery | | | | |
| Woodwork/Cookery | 36 | C- | Revision is needed before the external title. | |
| Metalwork/Needlework | 45 | C | Stuart has got plenty of confidence - but needs to revise to get a good grade. | |
| Engineering Drawing | | | | |
| Automobile Mechanics | 38 | B. | Stuart should do well, provided he revises thoroughly. | N |
| Design, Craft & Technology | | | | |
| Economics & Commerce / Computer Studies | | | | |
| Shorthand | 81 | B+ | Stuart has got his reward really well with a good result. | |
| Typewriting | | | | |
| Accounts | | | | |
| Office Practice | | | | |
| P.E./Games C.J.E | 86 | A | Excellent work throughout course. | JAR |

REMARKS Some reasonable performances. Now for that little extra effort in your weaker subjects between now + June.

_Philip Evans_  FORM TEACHER

CONDUCT V Good.

MARK or GRADE = Assessment of Achievement in Examinations or Tests  A = Ex
TERM'S WORK = Assessment of Effort and Achievement during Term  B = Ve

---

| Name | S. Cable | | |
|---|---|---|---|
| No. | Date 11/9/87 | £ | p |
| Wages | | 45 | — |
| Statutory sick pay | | | |
| **GROSS PAY £** | | 45 | — |
| Deductions: | | | |
| National Insurance | | 2 | 27 |
| Income Tax | | | |
| Total deductions | | 2 | 27 |
| Wages less deductions | | 42 | 73 |
| Income Tax refund | | | |
| **NET PAY £** | | 42 | 73 |

Please check immediately that contents agree with Net pay shown

One of my 'great' school reports and my first pay packet.

Check out the mullet on Kelly!

*Top*: Long haired lovers from Cwmaman…

*Below*: My first and only attempt at singing – this was the photo that reappeared as part of a pub quiz years later!

Oh my word…what was I thinking of?!!!

*Above*: My father's pride and joy and how I came up with the name 'Stereophonics'.

*Below*: Early photo of Tragic Love Company.

*Above*: (*from left*) Jeremy Pearce (V2 Records), Gareth Edwards, me and Ieuan Evans at the Morfa Stadium gig.

*Below*: Morfa stadium – what a great day!

One of our first gig flyers, and my 'access all areas' laminate from the U2 tour in 2001.

# The
# Stereophonics

**FORMERLY KNOWN AS TRAGIC LOVE COMPANY**

Catch us next at..........

CJ PROMOTION

## THE KING'S HEAD
## Fulham

4 Fulham High St
London SW6

## SUNDAY 3rd MARCH

On Stage 8.15PM
£ 3.50 with this flyer

call GGM

to seeing women in sparkling boob tops, smoking Woodbines, wearing white stilettos and dancing round their handbags. These girls − I *hope* they were girls, anyway − were beautiful. When the music stopped, they would all leap off the bar and come and sit next to the punters. It was feeding time at the zoo!

To be truthful, I wasn't interested in anything like that. We had been travelling for ages and it was raining as if there was no tomorrow. I just wanted to take the whole experience in. It was such an unbelievable place, not like anywhere else on the planet, including Amsterdam and Prague.

Kelly tapped me on the arm and said, 'Fuck! Look at him.'

I turned round to see our manager sitting in a booth with about six stunning Thai girls draped all over him as though he were a millionaire looking for a Thai bride. He had a grin on his face like that of a large Cheshire cat; he was lapping it up. I burst out laughing.

The girls were selling themselves for something like 400 bahts for a night of ultimate pleasure, which was about £20 in our money. I was half expecting they were giving him all the 'You wanna fucky-fucky?'

One girl plonked herself down by me and kept nudging me. 'Four hundred bahts, Four hundred bahts. Good night. Anything you want.'

I joked, 'How many Simpsons is it again?' I didn't want to know, but I bought her a drink to be friendly, and chatted.

She seemed quite offended. 'What you mean, you don't want me? Me not pretty?'

I explained that I thought she was very pretty, but I was married, and only there to have a drink.

She smirked and replied, 'Many married men have come to see me. Me very good.'

'I bet they have,' I replied, 'and I bet you are.'

We all had a few more drinks and a good laugh, then went back to the hotel to get ready for the filming the next day. Making the video was a riot: we mimed to the song in a monsoon while helicopters flew overhead, bombs went off all around us and 1,000 mad members of the Thai army were standing in the rain dancing like fools. They were the campest set of soldiers I have ever seen; they would have looked more at home dancing in a gay bar to the Pet Shop Boys.

The funniest thing I remember about the entire trip was Kelly and his phone bill. I must explain that everything in Thailand was so cheap it was unbelievable. We couldn't *give* our money away. It was cheap as chips, as they say. So, come the day we had to book out of the hotel, Kelly really showed our small-town valley mentality. He was handed a bill for about £2,000 for using the phone in his room. He was gobsmacked; he explained to us that he thought that, because everything else was so cheap, phoning home would be, too. He had been on the blower to his new girlfriend most of the time and had run up a massive bill. He hit the roof, yelling and shouting at the poor receptionist. He was jumping up and down, which looked hilarious because no one could see the small fucker from behind the big oak desk. John got involved. I laughed so hard that I think I actually pissed myself.

At first he said no, he wasn't paying, but I think in the end they settled on somewhere around £1,500.

'Write a song about that, Kel,' I yelled at him. 'How about: "I Refused to Pay My Phone Bill"?'

## PERFORMANCE AND JACKBOOTS

I always found doing the videos enjoyable, but hard work. Not hard work like the working-down-a-coal-mine type of labour, though. To say that would be unfair to people who actually work for a living. There's just so much time spent hanging around waiting while people discuss this shot and that shot, or waiting for make-up artists, that it's maddening. And there are also some really early mornings, sitting around the location after the obligatory late nights, sampling the local brew.

We were filming the video for 'Just Looking' up in Scotland and, as normal, it was freezing. The plan had been to finish it off, catch a train down to London, then have two days off before flying out to Japan for a short, sharp tour. But plans are there to be broken, as they say, and we got hit with a blizzard, the great-grandmother of all blizzards, actually. The electricians refused to work because of the weather conditions. They downed their tools and all fucked off home. It brought back memories of starting the union in my brother's old factory, so for a short while 'Stuart the Red' could sympathise with them. At first it was a good laugh, getting snowed in with several barrels of Guinness and lots of bottles of your finest Scotch whisky. What could be better? So we made the most of it and got hammered and had a great laugh. But then the clock started ticking and conditions didn't get any better.

Plan B was to phone a studio in London and finish off making the video there. It was all arranged. We got on an overnight train from Glasgow, which arrived in London at six in the morning. We had a quick freshen-up at the hotel, then went straight to the studio to finish the bloody thing. It eventually took us a day and a half. Then, as soon as it was in the can, we got into cars heading straight to the airport and onto a twelve-hour flight to the Land of the Rising Sun.

I was really grumpy. I hadn't slept properly for three days. We argued and bickered all the way there. And who said rock stars have it easy? Give me a bloody fly press and two million metal things to squash by the end of my shift any day!

The success of the album opened a lot of doors for us. The summer of 1999 was massive for us as far as playing live was concerned. We were performing at most of the big summer festivals and supporting some big, big names, but we wanted to do something special back home in Wales. We organised our own little show on 31 July in a place called the Morfa Stadium. It was a sports stadium. Maybe *stadium* was too strong a word to describe it; it was more of a big running track with a large stand at the one end. Anyway, it was going to be knocked down and developed into the new Liberty Stadium football and rugby venue for the two successful teams of Swansea.

We got the idea for the show because we had always talked about playing a concert that people would remember in years to come. Kind of like the first Live Aid concert. We wanted people to say, 'Remember the day the 'Phonics played at the Morfa Stadium? Well, I was there, and it was brilliant.' And I think we weren't that far off the mark, because if you had asked people before the gig where the Morfa Stadium was, I bet you more than 80 per cent wouldn't have known. But now, because of that day, at least 50,000 can tell you where it was and what a great concert they saw there.

It was a celebration of being Welsh; a big thank-you for all the fans, old and new, who had supported us and were proud that we were from their neck of the woods. And it wasn't just about our music. There were all kinds of events that went on throughout the day: such as five-a-side football matches, a tug-o'-war competition, a seven-a-side rugby tournament and boxing. There was a showground and food stalls; it was the complete package. And there were lots of stars milling around, such as Joe Calzaghe, Melinda Messenger, Gareth Edwards, Ian Rush and many more.

It was the scariest and most nerve-racking, yet most enjoyable, time of my life. I remember all week praying for it to be fine. 'Please, please, be sunny, please don't rain.' I kept looking up at the heavens and checking the weather forecast every few minutes. I've been to festivals where it's pissed down all day and it's no fun. Of course there are the diehards who will insist that the bad weather doesn't spoil these events at all, but to me it fucking well does. There's nothing better than lying on the grass with a can of cold lager in one hand, a joint in your mouth, listening to music with the sun on your back. It's miles better than all the bollocks of standing there grouped together like penguins on an iceberg, freezing cold, soaking wet and trying to enjoy it while singing along to some bloke on stage who's covered by a tarpaulin.

Thankfully, on the day of the event, the gods were really smiling widely on us. It turned out to be absolutely glorious. We couldn't have ordered it better if we'd tried. Obviously, being a typical Welsh person, the pessimistic side of me kicked in as soon as I knew it was going to be sunny. 'What if it's *too* hot? What if everyone flakes out on us? Should we spray everyone down with water? What if the stage melts?' I thought I'd end up going round the bend.

## DEMONS AND COCKTAILS

The night before, and the night of the gig, we stayed at the Marriott Hotel in Swansea. The night before, we were all nervous and had a few drinks in the bar. Kelly went to bed. I've never been one to go to bed early before a gig. I knew I would only be up all night staring at the paint peeling off the walls, and I needed a drink to relax me and put me in the mood, so Richard and I sneaked out on the tiles. We went to see a Manic Street Preachers tribute band. We had a great craic, talking to all the fans and really chilling out.

During the build-up to the day, we sat up in a box overlooking the arena. I sat there watching all these people piling in. 'Fucking hell's bells, this is big! This is massive.' My nerves were on edge; I couldn't stop talking or bouncing about. The day dragged on and on. Waiting to get out on stage seemed to last several lifetimes.

Then it was time to walk out. It was something special, a completely different world: the noise, the flag-waving, the sight of thousands and thousands of people, all there to see us. How mental is that? Twenty months before, we couldn't fill a telephone box, and now all this. I, being the height of fashion and the guru of style that I am, decided to wear a flat cap. It was my own tribute to the great Bonnie Scott, but everyone in the stadium thought I was trying to copy Andy Capp from the newspaper cartoon. I don't know why I bother sometimes!

The show was awesome. Being on stage and listening to 50,000 fans singing our songs, word for word, was really quite amazing. There were tears in my eyes, a lump at the back of my throat and a smile on my face as wide as the Golden Gate Bridge.

To add to the 'Celebrate Being Welsh' theme, before the first encore we had a huge screen showing Welsh heroes, past and present, such as Tom Jones, Richard Burton, Shirley Bassey, Anthony Hopkins and other great Welsh stars. We finished the sequence with some clips of a series of great rugby tries from Scott Gibbs, Gareth Edwards and others.

During the first encore, Kelly sang a song called, 'As Long as We Beat the English'. This was a song that he had been asked to write for the Welsh rugby match in the Six Nations Championship against England. It was based on a series of mini cartoons aired on the BBC, where, in the last episode, an animated Graham Henry asked an animated version of the Stereophonics to write a song to help them beat the old enemy, England, in the next game. It was all meant to be tongue-in-cheek. I remember Kelly writing it while we were rehearsing one day. It was based on the old Welsh mindset that it was okay if we got smashed by any other country in the world, so long as we beat the English. I can imagine it to be a similar type of scenario in Scotland and Ireland, and probably the rest of the world. The clip of Kelly singing it was played during the week of the big game on BBC Wales. Again it was meant to be just a bit of friendly banter.

But when Kelly played the song at the gig, it all backfired. Some non-Welsh people thought that the song, plus all the cheering and hollering to the film clips, was a show of nationalism. It was blown out of all perspective when, supposedly, someone wrote in to the *New Musical Express* saying they had been scared for their life among a massive horde of drunken, flag-waving Welsh. They equated it to a Nazi rally.

Call me slightly biased, but I thought the observations were outrageous and unfair. If a journalist had written about any other part of the British Isles like that, or a minority race in Britain, there would have been a fucking uproar. To compare Welsh people at a peaceful musical event to flag-waving Nazis at a Nuremberg rally was right out of order. I am more than convinced that 100 per cent of the people in that stadium on that day were there to have a good time, a few beers, a couple of hot dogs, sing a couple of songs, maybe try and get a love bite or two, and go home happy. I don't think anyone was really looking to put on a pair of bloody jackboots and go goose-stepping across the Severn Bridge with the intention of invading Bristol, singing several choruses of 'Roll Up and Shine'. There was only one arrest in a crowd of 50,000 people. *One* arrest. Surely, that must be a world record. Where's Norris McWhirter when you need him?

I think the concert deserved more than the negative press it was given. Even today, it upsets me when I think of the headlines. For God's sake, give us a break. It was supposed to be a rock'n'roll show, nothing more, nothing less. I can't remember the name of the journalist, which really doesn't matter, because, if there's justice in the world, he's flipping burgers now in McDonald's with a gold star on his chest for having the most zits.

At the end of the day, some of these so-called 'journalists' and the stuff they write are not worth the bother to get upset over. I swear, some of them leave university with a degree in 'know fuck all'. They buy a Blur CD, get a rock-star haircut and suddenly they think they know the history of rock'n'roll. I remember a guy came to interview us from one of the music rags and he had never heard of Neil Young – never heard of him. Even my Aunt Joan had heard of him! I thought, 'How can you sit there and interview us if you don't know who someone like that is?' Shouldn't there be a basic music test that they should have to pass? Some type of journo examination?

First question: Who sang 'Heartbreak Hotel'?

1. Elvis Presley
2. Elvis Costello
3. Donald Trump
4. The Holiday Inn and the All-Day Buffets

It's just basic stuff that people in that position – people in a position to ruin someone's livelihood – should know. How can you have 'music journalist' on your business card and not know who Neil Young is? You would hope that someone working in a comprehensive school teaching geography would have a fair idea how an oxbow lake was formed, even if they had never seen one in real life.

At the time of all the fuss, Kelly was going out with a girl who worked in the *NME* offices and we were so pissed off with the reaction to the concert in their paper that we talked about getting the key off her and going to the offices and splattering paint everywhere. We never did, but if someone had driven us there we would have done it, without a shadow of a doubt.

It pissed me off almost as much as the time the press called us 'meat-and-two-veg boys from Wales, who loved their AC/DC in large amounts'. I don't see anything wrong with liking AC/DC, but they made us out to be some kind of idiots not only for liking them, but for admitting it with pride. Three years later, Angus Young was on the front cover of *NME* with the headline, THE

GREATEST ROCK STAR OF ALL TIME IN THE GREATEST BAND. So it was okay for them to say how good the band was when it sold them 100,000 copies. All of a sudden, people were walking around thinking they were cool in their brand new AC/DC T-shirts. I bet most of them would struggle to name three of their songs. Before that, AC/DC were nothing but a joke to them. Don't get me wrong, I think there are some real good journalists out there who really know their stuff, but there are some real pathetic ones who make the whole group look bad, too.

After the gig at the Morfa Stadium had finished, I recall standing there watching the fireworks display going off high up in the dark Welsh sky over the city. John looked pleased and said, 'What a great display! Well worth 15 grand.'

I nearly choked on my beer. 'Fifteen fuckin' grand? Are you joking me? We didn't pay 15 fucking grand for a big box of squibs – did we?'

He smiled and told me it was all part of the bigger plan and, to be fair to him, he was right.

After the show we went back to the hotel and had one hell of a party. It had been only a year since the successful Cardiff Castle gig to 10,000 people and now we had taken it up another level or five, thanks to John. This time in the hotel bar there was no need for any big stars. It was just us, our families, an open bar and the sight of the sea rolling in on the Swansea coastline.

To put the icing on my cake, in the morning I found myself over sixty grand richer – not bad for a chopsey twat with a GCSE in metalwork.

Another great experience for us around that time was getting to play with some of our heroes. We were asked to play at the

## PERFORMANCE AND JACKBOOTS

Toxic Twin Towers Ball at Wembley Stadium in 1999. We were on the bill with the great Aerosmith – or the Smith of Aero, as we jokingly called them – the Black Crowes and Lenny Kravitz. When we were starting out, we had proudly done covers of all of them and now we were going to perform on the same stage. How bizarre is that?

During the gig, we must have made an impression on the Aerosmith guys because they invited us to do some more shows with them across Europe.

We were also invited to play a charity gig at Café de Paris in London the night after the Wembley gig with Jimmy Page. Again, we were in fine company: all the bands from the Toxic Twin show were there to perform, along with many others. Sitting opposite us was the brilliant Billy Duffy from the Cult. I loved the Cult; I don't know how many people appreciated just how big they were. To put it in perspective, Guns N' Roses used to support them at one time in the States. I still couldn't believe we were mingling in the company of legends. We were like naïve little kids – we wouldn't have looked out of place in short trousers and blazers, with satchels on our backs. But, to our advantage, the venue was small and suited us down to the ground. If anyone in the club didn't know us before we went on, they definitely did by the time we finished. We rocked the place to its core. Steven Tyler stood there nodding his head. 'Good show, man. Good show.'

Jimmy asked us to sign a guitar that was going to be auctioned off and we had a photo with the great man taken by his daughter Scarlet, who later became a good friend of the band and took many great photos of us. By then, I'd had a few beers and I really wanted to speak to Billy Duffy. He was the top man in my eyes. I moved in close to him like a stalker. I didn't know what to say to him and I knew whatever I said would come out total wank. I would probably stutter and say something completely stupid like, 'Hi, Billy, you don't sweat much for a rock god.'

Finally, I built up enough courage to approach him. 'Hey Billy, my name's Stuart Cable from the Stereophonics. I'm a big fan.'

Surprisingly he said, 'Hey, man, love the band, great sound.'

I was shocked, blown over. We started talking and I told him we used to play 'Wild Flower' when we were starting out.

'Fuck off, man!' He seemed genuinely pleased. I could tell he was itching to play. 'Fancy having a knock?' he asked.

I thought I was hearing things. '*What*?'

'Come on, let's go and play it.'

I called Kelly over to tell him. We were both speechless. How many people in the world get the chance to play a song with their rock hero?

Billy went to see if he could organise it.

'Do you know the words, Kel?' I asked the obvious question.

'I know some of them.'

We had to think fast. We sat at the bar and wrote the words out on a napkin. Billy came back; he had sorted it. We walked out on stage. The three of us and the super-cool Billy Duffy. Billy had borrowed one of Kelly's guitars and it was so funny seeing him struggle to lower the strap.

We learnt a big lesson that night. You never give someone like Duffy one of Kelly's guitars. In fact, you don't give Kelly's guitar to anyone other than some bloke who doesn't mind getting shot out of a cannon.

## PERFORMANCE AND JACKBOOTS

It was wrapped around Billy's neck like a hangman's noose. He finally managed to lower it as low as it could go; he had always been someone who wore his guitar low down, a guitar slinger. He looked at the audience, then at me.

'Ready?' he asked.

'Yeah,' I nodded back.

He placed his foot on the monitor and suddenly blasted out the opening notes on his guitar. The sound shot out at a hundred and eighty miles per hour. I was pumping. The hairs on the back of my neck were standing on end. Then Kelly's rough, brilliant voice kicked in as if it belonged on the track. The song went down a storm. It was a highlight of my life that I will never forget, and hopefully one day I will do it again with the great man, because to me Billy Duffy *is* the Wild Flower.

We played the Aerosmith gig in Holland the following weekend. During the sound check they came backstage, surrounded by a posse of big black bouncers. Everywhere they went, the bouncers followed. They sat with us and we started talking. Being the big AC/DC fan that I am, and knowing they had toured with AC/DC in their early days, I mentioned it to Steven Tyler.

'Hey, Joe,' he shouted across the room to Joe Perry. 'When did we tour with AC/DC, was it '74, '75 or '76?' It must have been around the time of their full-on rock'n'roll excess, so I assumed their minds were a little cloudy.

I knew exactly when it was. 'It was '76,' I replied sheepishly.

They all looked at me, and I could see them thinking about it.

'I think he's right, man.' Joe nodded at me.

That night when we went on, Steven Tyler and Joe Perry

watched us from the side of the stage. It was so intimidating. I caught Kelly's attention; he looked across at them. I'm sure his little legs buckled under the weight of their stares. We were all nervous. When we came off, Steven stopped me. 'Liked the show, man. And by the way, I didn't realise how good AC/DC really is.' Apparently he had been listening to them all afternoon in his room. Later that night, we met up again and talked for ages about past groups and other stuff. He was a top bloke.

Before our next concert, I asked Steven if it would be okay to watch them perform from the side of the stage later that night. He told me it would be no problem and asked one of his bouncers to sort it out. I was really looking forward to it. Chris Robinson, from the Black Crowes, and I headed for the stage. It wasn't as easy to get there as I expected. We had to go through about ten different sets of bouncers, who seemed to get bigger and meaner the nearer we got to the band. It was harder than trying to get into Russia without a visa. Finally we made it. Chris rolled a joint and we got ready to watch the cream of America strut their stuff. A huge bouncer came over and grunted, 'Oh, don't forget: you can't look him in the eye when he's performing.'

'Who?' We both looked confused.

'Mr Tyler. You can't look Mr Tyler in the eye when he's performing. He doesn't like it.'

'*What*?'

He stared. 'No looking him directly in the eye, understand?' He stomped away.

Chris shrugged his shoulders at me. I was thinking, 'Why can't I look him in the eye? Will I turn to stone? Will *he* turn to stone?

Will he melt like the witch in *The Wizard of Oz*?' My mind was doing cartwheels.

I stood back and watched them blast through their set. They were awesome, so much power. Then, about four songs into their set, I think they were playing, 'Love in an Elevator', when Steven, with his head facing the floor, sauntered our way. I was thinking, 'What the fuck am I going to do?' The scene seemed to play out in slow motion. Without warning, he looked up quickly and stared straight at us. Unbelievably, everyone on the sidelines instantly turned the other way, in perfect unison. It was mad. I dared not look, but I can only assume he must have stood there, smiling at us all wickedly, before joining the rest of the band.

How mad is that? What power one person has to make grown men do something like that, for no logical reason. I always thought after that show of power that he was at the top of the pecking order when it came to superstars. Surely he was the one everyone looked up to. But my image was shattered the night we were at the MTV Music Awards with Richard Branson in New York. Aerosmith were there and they were sitting near us. Sorry, *we* were sitting near *them*. Tommy Lee and the ultra-sexy Pamela Anderson were sitting near us as well.

Steven called me over. He lowered his sunglasses and asked me, 'Hey, Stu, how far would you stick your head up Pamela Anderson's ass?'

I burst out laughing and said, 'All the way, Steve.'

He sniggered like a little schoolboy and muttered, 'Me too.' And he walked off grinning. He was the king in my eyes.

After the event we went to the Virgin Party at the Four Seasons Hotel. It was like a who's who of the rock and glamour world, wall-to-wall superstars. We just happened to be talking to David Bowie. I'll say that again, in case you didn't read it properly. We were casually chatting away to *David Bowie*, when Steven Tyler came over. He flicked David's hair and said something like, 'Hey David, what are you doing with your hair? You and your wife look like rockers.'

Bowie, as cool as a cucumber, replied, 'I'm trying to be the David Beckham of rock'n'roll.'

Steven looked confused. 'The *who* of *what*?'

Bowie winked at me and Kelly, and joked, 'They'll tell you.' And then he sauntered off, cool as fuck, sipping a glass of wine.

That was the moment I started to realise there was also a pecking order with the stars. There were the A, B, C and D lists of celebrities, but above all of them came the G list: the gods. At the time we were probably near the bottom of the pile. Above us were the stars, then the real stars, then the superstars, but it didn't stop there. At the top were the gods, the individuals even the superstars looked up to, the ones who made everyone go weak at the knees. After the Beckham comment, I knew that David Bowie was, and still is, firmly in the god category. Very few could touch him.

We met another god that night, Paul McCartney, who told us that he was a fan of the band, which was hard to appreciate. *The* Paul McCartney, a fan of our little band. Could we ever get a bigger compliment? It was like a dream. In one night I had met two gods, several superstars, numerous stars, and many celebrities, and what's more, I had the vivid picture of me sticking my head up the rear end of the delicious Pamela Anderson.

Now life doesn't get much better than that!

## BEST GIGS I'VE PLAYED IN (SO FAR)

MORFA STADIUM: It was a huge gig for us, off the scale, and it all went perfectly: the three S's: sun, sound and Stereophonics. And on top of that, we each made around sixty grand for doing something I loved. I bought my first house in Cwmaman out of it. What a job!

CARDIFF CASTLE: Every time I drive through the capital and see the big old castle staring back at me it makes me feel so proud to know that my mates and I conquered it for two hours – and I have the DVD to prove it.

DUBLIN SLANE CASTLE: We supported Robbie Williams there and only two years later, we headlined it ourselves. This was proper rock-star shit. After the gig, there were waiting limos stocked with champagne. U2 were watching us, and 80,000 insane Irish people singing word for word.

MADISON SQUARE GARDEN: Here we were supporting U2. It was a week after September 11. We had a ball. Not only supporting the biggest band in the world, but playing in a place with such history. And what a party after!

READING FESTIVAL: This just about beats headlining the almighty Glastonbury, mainly because we were paid a ridiculous sum of money for fucking about on stage. And, let me tell you, it *was* a ridiculous sum of money, but I wasn't complaining.

# CHAPTER 6

# WHOLE LOTTA TOURING

**M**y son Cian was born around the time we really started to do proper tours. And what I mean by 'proper' is just turning up for the sound check and playing the gig instead of having to do all the ball-breaking rigmarole of setting up the gear and then taking it down again, or walking around the audience after the show handing out leaflets for the next gig. His birth was the most exciting night of my life outside the band, and of course my wedding night. I remember it as if it were only yesterday.

It was around 2am on a wet Thursday night when Nicola's waters broke. We were still living in Cwmaman at the time. We jumped in the car and drove to Cardiff's Heath Hospital.

Surprisingly, Nicola was quite calm during the 30-minute journey. It was I who went over the edge. I talked nonstop the entire way there, in a panic. She had planned to have a water birth, but after she'd spent quite some time in the water we knew that wasn't going to work out. She was 18 hours in labour. Can you imagine how she would have looked if she had stayed in the tub for that long? Like a crinkled chip, that's how.

I can't imagine how rough it must have been on her because it was hard enough on me. I paced around the delivery room and lived every contraction as if I were having them myself. They gave her gas and air and an epidural, which really seemed to help her. Unfortunately, it didn't do anything for me. I was still a basket case. The labour seemed to go on for ever. Just when I thought he was never going to appear, out he popped. I was crying my eyes out as I cut the umbilical cord and held him in my arms. It was the proudest moment of my life.

When I left the hospital, I couldn't wait to go and tell everyone about my son. Just like my dad, and probably his dad before him, I went to the pub and got plastered. There's not a better feeling in the world than sitting in the Ivy Bush surrounded by your mates and family straight after you've just witnessed the birth of your child. It got even more emotional with every free drink that went down. I ended up crying again like a baby as I bragged to everyone how beautiful he was.

And I still think he's the most beautiful child in the world. He has always been a great kid, even though he didn't sleep tidy for the first five years of his life. Nicola is a great mum and was great with him. Especially getting up in the middle of the night when he had bad colic. I was useless. Once I fall asleep, wild horses trampling on my chest can't wake me up.

I adored him from the first second I saw him, but when he started to walk and talk was the best time for me. He became my best buddy. Up until then, he was just a pissing, shitting, eating and spewing machine. I know that's probably a man thing to say, but after about 18 months he really started to come alive and turn into this little person with a mind and a personality of his own.

I remember when he was just a little thing and we took him to Disneyland in Paris. We were watching the parade when a few people came up to me and asked for either a photograph or an autograph. Cian turned and said, 'Dad, does Mickey Mouse know you?'

'Of course, son,' I joked. 'He's even got a Stuart Cable watch.'

Cian's presence in my life really made the experience of touring a roller-coaster ride of emotion. Sometimes I really loved being on the road, especially at the beginning of a new tour. It was exciting. There were different sets, new songs, new venues, new after-show rider lists. A rider list is a list of all the things real rock stars have the venue make ready for them after the show. I remember the excitement the first time we provided our rider list to the concert hall. Being typically Welsh, I didn't think the stuff would be there, or someone else would nick it, but I was wrong. Unlike the megastars who spend a fortune for weird and outrageous after-show titbits such as caviar on toast and dancing midgets, we were never extravagant in our selection, mainly because, in the end, we had to pay for it.

Our rider list didn't have any real strange stuff on it. It normally consisted of the following:

- 4 x bottles of Hooch (must have been trying to impress the ladies)
- 16 x good-quality lager (there was no weak shit for us)
- 4 x bottles of cider
- 1 x bottle of vodka

- 2 x litre bottles of still mineral water (must have been a mistake)
- 2 x fresh orange juice (usually to mix with the vodka)
- 6 x hot meals, 1 being vegetarian

The group Skunk Anansie used to insist that there be 4 clean pairs of white socks in their dressing room after they got off stage. I thought they were just trying to show how bizarre they were, a bit like a watered-down version of Michael Jackson. But I found out later that they wanted the socks to wear in the shower so they didn't get foot fungus. I guess there was logic in their madness!

But the novelty of the new sets and rider lists wore off rather quickly as I started to think of Cian and getting back to God's own country. Watching him grow had made me realise just how much I missed my dad and evoked a fear of leaving my son in the same drastic circumstances as my brother and I had been left. I wanted to be able to watch him grow up and teach him about life, teach him how to swim and do all the things that my father wasn't able to do for me. My fear of not being there to share Cian's life into adulthood was probably one of the main reasons I hated to fly so much, and why I counted down the days to the end of the tour.

I felt like a hamster running on a wheel. We were the biggest band in the UK and all Simon and I could think about was the number of days left to go home. Simon was Kelly's guitar technician; he was one of the guys we insisted on bringing on board as we started to tour.

'Do you know what night this is, Stu?' he would ask me before the show.

'Amsterdam, our second show?'

'No.' He would be checking our schedule. 'It's only 15 shows left before we get to go home.' He would mark it off on a big calendar. We would go through the same routine every night until the last one.

That's how extraordinary the whole thing had become. All roads led back home and I couldn't wait to get there. Looking back now, I can't believe how stupid and ridiculous that really was. I wasn't making parts on a fly press: I was performing in front of thousands of adoring fans who had paid good money to come and see a rock'n'roll show. It was the best job in the world and all I could think of was lying on my settee, eating cheese on toast and drinking a mug of tea and watching some boring soap show on TV.

But I would be lying if I said I didn't get bored with that just as quickly as I got bored with touring; there's just no pleasing people like me sometimes. I would get home, spend a few days living a family life again – playing with Cian, mowing the lawn, relaxing, recharging my batteries – and would soon start wishing I was on the road again. In total, it probably took about three days maximum before I became restless. I'm not sure if people can appreciate just how difficult it is trying to settle back into a normal way of life after playing in front of thousands of fans, night after night, meeting superstars backstage, living in five-star hotels, ordering room service, doing drugs, drink and more drink.

Always around the fourth day at home while sitting there with Nicola and Cian, I would start watching the clock. In my mind I was already reliving the excitement of the gigs, waiting for that special tap on the stage door, the knock that indicated we had five minutes before show time. Although I was in my living room, I still got the adrenaline rush as I pictured myself looking into Kelly's or Richard's eyes before walking out into the spotlight.

Surrounding ourselves with people we could trust and rely on – and those who would count down the days till the end of the tour with me, as Simon did – made the touring process a lot more comfortable. It was one of the first things we insisted on. Simon was great at his job and was also one of our biggest party animals. I guess he was in good company. Once in France he got so pissed that he wandered off and we found him three days later in hospital. The tale went that he had been drugged, kidnapped and beaten up. Well, that was his side of the story, anyway.

We hired Julian to drive us about at first, and then he later became the band's photographer. He was always classed as the odd-job man. He would do anything from selling T-shirts to making coffee.

Dave was the sound engineer, who in a previous life had been a very good hairdresser. Although he would never admit it, I think he was glad we had saved him from a lifetime of snipping scissors, sweeping up hair and giving scruff cuts to customers with greasy tresses.

Swampy became my drum tech. He was brilliant and became a great mate. Kelly's brother, Kevin, became the tour manager. I don't think there was any nepotism in his appointment. I was told he was offered the role because he had once driven to North Wales without the aid of a Sat Nav system or a map, and he also knew the capital of Peru. I always wanted to ask him if he knew how an oxbow lake was formed, but I didn't want to put him under too much pressure; he was under enough as it was. Kevin was a nice guy who was good to have around, and worked hard in difficult situations.

They became our core team. They shared all of our ups and downs, and we had a brilliant laugh along the way. Most occasions were like a rugby tour or a stag weekend – a stag weekend that lasted up to ten months sometimes and took us to some weird and wonderful places in the world.

The work was hard for the boys, and, to be honest, we paid them peanuts for the pleasure. We relied on the after-show partying, which normally lasted all night, to make up for it. There was lots of dope floating about, stacks of booze all mixed together with plenty of honest Welsh working-class humour. And, surprisingly, Julian, who always had an eye for the ladies anyway, was really the only one at that time with any girls hanging around him. And that's only because it's an essential element required for a first-class photographer. Unlike with some bands, it really wasn't about how many birds we could pull. I think we were too much into the music and the odd spliff to be distracted by all that.

I remember one of the first times we played in the States. We were performing in Lamont Pike in upstate New York with the '80s ska band The Specials, from Coventry. Later, in the dressing room, one of the band members asked if we would like a little weed. We were never ones to turn down a free smoke, so we nodded our heads politely. He handed us half a carrier bag full of the stuff. They were flying home the next morning and didn't want to risk smuggling it back. There were enough drugs in the carrier bag to fuel a train to fucking Las Vegas and back, without stopping … it was going to be one hell of a night. We all stared at it as if it were a bomb about to explode. We didn't know what we were going to do with the stuff. Perhaps we should have employed a bloody drug technician to be part of our core team to help us out. I could see the advert in the local paper.

> **WANTED – Drug Technician to travel world with up-and-coming rock'n'roll band. No formal qualifications required, but knowledge of strange substances essential. Must be trustworthy. Lots of pockets in coat desirable.**
> **[end display text]**

The queue for the interview would have stretched from Aberdare town centre to the docks in Aberdeen.

We were due to fly to LA ourselves the next day, so we decided the only thing we could do was to smoke as much as we could that night. Richard was chief roller and manufactured some of the biggest joints in history; we needed at least two people to hold them. Even Bob Marley would have struggled to finish one of Richard's spliffs. We smoked to our hearts' content. At first I'd never giggled so much in my life; my sides were hurting. Then we got lost in our very own ghost town. We all ended up wrecked. If my memory serves me correctly, Simon was the worst for wear yet again. He was on the bog most of the night, white as a sheet. He had stuff coming out of every orifice in his body. I have never seen anyone's spew shoot so far across the room in my life since the girl in *The Exorcist*.

I wasn't much better. I remember trying to get to the safety of my room but the corridor was getting longer and longer with every step. It must have taken me an age to get there. Unfortunately, the spins hit me before I could get through my door. The spins must be the worst thing ever invented by God. What a terrible feeling! Spew City followed for me as well shortly after – and without the aid of a brown-paper bag. I did leave the cleaning lady a large tip for the inconvenience and to cover the cost of the extra bottle of cleaner she had to use.

In the morning I was completely fucked. Swampy pushed me down to reception on one of those luggage carts. I still claim you can't call yourself a proper rock star unless you have been pushed out of a lift on a luggage cart with eyes like pissholes in the snow. I'm not sure how the hell we made it to LA that day, but we did.

LA was a great time but the tension of touring was taking its toll on us. I remember that Kelly and I had a massive argument in the house of Adam Duritz, lead singer with the Counting Crows. Adam turned out to be a fan of the band and one night, after we played in the Viper Room, Johnny Depp's place, Adam invited us back to his pad for a meal. He lived in David Niven's old house in Laurel Canyon, up in the Hollywood Hills. How cool is that, to be able to say to visitors, 'Oh, yes, David Niven, the British actor, used to live here.'

As soon as I walked in, I could feel the elegance and style of the place. I could picture the old actor strolling around in his smoking jacket and silk scarf, with a cigarette in its holder. What a contrast to the place we were staying in! We were camped out in a rough part of LA, and I mean brutal. Some places in Wales pretend to be tough with their skinheads, bulldogs and burnt-out cars, but this was something else. Proper violent. Even the cockroaches wore bulletproof vests and carried guns.

Adam insisted on making us his famous signature dish, Dr Pepper ribs. Apparently he boiled the ribs in a frying pan covered in the famous Dr Pepper beverage before he cooked them. It sounded terrible, but tasted wonderful. I would recommend it to anyone. After the meal we all got drunker and drunker, and smoked a little Bob Hope to help pass the time away.

Later on I took a walk alone about the house to clear my head. I looked at my watch and realised that Nicola would probably be awake back in the UK, so I had a brainwave to give her a call. I found a phone and walked around as I called her. I ended up in the basement, in a massive workout gym. Normally I would run, or walk, in the opposite direction as fast as I could, but drugs sometimes play tricks with my mind, so I sat on an exercise bike, peddling backwards for some strange reason while talking to my wife about the tour and how I had a brand-new recipe that I couldn't wait to show her when I got back home.

We talked for a while and just as I hung up, Kelly stormed into the room. 'What the fuck you doing?' he grunted at me.

'*What?*' I nearly fell off the bike.

'I've been looking for you for ages. Who were you on the phone to?'

'None of your business. Now fuck off!'

He was in a wicked mood. 'I hope you weren't phoning your missus back in Wales.'

'What's it to do with you who I'm phoning?' I was bouncing.

We were like two little kids standing in the schoolyard.

'It's taking the piss, that's all. It's going to cost him a fortune.'

I looked around at the surroundings. 'He doesn't give a fuck. How much is he worth? He lives in Laurel Canyon in David Niven's old house, for fuck's sake! He's shagging Courtney fucking Cox,' I yelled back at him.

For anyone on the outside looking in, we must have appeared like an old married couple. We continued to shout at each other for a while, and then he stormed off back upstairs. I clambered off the bike and followed him. I told his brother to get him out of my face, otherwise I was going to kill him. I was breathing fire. Adam hadn't really noticed anything was going on. He was just chilling out and listening to music.

We left in several taxis at around two, and of course I didn't go back to the hotel room. I needed more drink. We were due to fly to Australia on the Monday morning, so my aim was to get hammered and have a nice lie-in on the Sunday, our day off. When I finally clambered into bed, I put my earplugs in because Simon was the loudest snorer I have ever shared a room with. He could snore for Wales! It was incredible.

Next thing I remember, Simon was shaking me quite violently around nine o'clock on Sunday morning.

'Go away, Simon.'

'Butt, butt, we've got to go – quick.'

My head was bumping, my throat dry. 'It's Sunday. What are you on about?'

'There's been a screw-up. We're flying to Australia today.'

His words hit me like a cold glass of water to the face. I leapt out of bed. Okay, that was a lie: I crawled out of bed like an old guy with 150 pounds of piles. Our room was a mess. We had wet washing hanging up on the backs of chairs and doors. Simon raced to the laundry room to see if he could get the stuff dried.

I went into Kelly's room to see what the hell was going on. Of course he was sitting there all packed with a smug look on his face. We didn't say anything. His brother explained that the international travel agent who worked for the record company had fucked up big time and had got the dates mixed up.

I glanced out of the window and pointed. 'I don't think we're going anywhere,' I said. Outside the streets were gridlocked because they had just started the LA Marathon.

They all looked out. The streets were packed, diversions everywhere.

I felt like shit and went back to my room to get my stuff together. I couldn't believe it; I needed a day in bed recovering, not flying to another part of the bloody world. I had a shower to wake myself up. When I finally got down to the lobby, there was no one there, not a soul. They had all left me.

'What a bunch of wankers!' I grunted. 'What am I going to do now?' Then the old Dunkirk spirit took over. 'Right, I'll show them. I'll get to the bloody airport if it's the last thing I do!' I raced out into the sunlight, not the best thing in the world for a hangover.

I hailed a cab. 'Hey, driver, if you get me to the airport quickly, there's an extra 20 dollars in it for you. Don't spare the horses.'

He bombed towards the airport, but it was slow progress for much of the journey. All the major roads had been blocked off. We eventually reached the freeway, but then disaster struck.

'Hey, butt,' I whispered, 'you'll have to pull over for a minute.' He looked at me, confused.

I must have looked quite sheepish in his rear view mirror.

'Sorry, mate, but I need to have a shit.' I was normally as regular as clockwork, but all the rushing around and added stress had messed up my insides. He slammed on the brakes.

I clambered out of the car. There I was, on a grass verge by the side of the freeway, trousers around my ankles, taking a dump. There were cars bleeping, trucks blowing their horns, and, worst of all, people were slowing down to give it some rubbernecking. Later on, I was thinking how funny it would have been if I had caused a major car pile-up:

> **LA news: 'Today, 17 people were killed in a major car pile-up as they all stopped to watch some UK rock star with outrageously curly hair letting it rip on the freeway. One eyewitness describes the scene: 'It was terrible. I'm not sure what he'd eaten, but I'm sure I saw sweetcorn!'**

Finally, I got to the terminal with about two nanoseconds to spare. They were actually closing the doors when I raced up. I was still hungover something rotten; I swore I was never going to drink again. Kelly and I were still not talking, and luckily for me, the plane wasn't full and they had spread us around. I was sitting halfway back in the middle section. Tony, our organist, was just behind me. I assumed Kelly was somewhere up near the front, although he was so small I couldn't see his head above the seats. Richard and the crew were at the back, already fast asleep.

I was still quite upset that they left me at the hotel, but relieved I had actually made it. I couldn't wait for the plane to take off so

I could stretch out across the seats and get some shut-eye. I worked out that I must have had a total of three hours' sleep over the two days. I was cream-crackered and over the moon that there no one was sitting beside me.

Everything was going to plan until I saw a man and woman rushing up the aisle in my direction. I turned to Tony. 'I bet they're going to sit here.'

He laughed and muttered in his thick North-of-England accent, 'I bet they fucking do, Twiggy.' He always called me Twiggy, because of my athletic figure and little beer pot.

The guy stopped in front of me. 'G'day, matey.' He held out his hand. He looked like Alf Stewart from the Australian soap *Neighbours*.

Inside I could hear myself screaming, 'No, God, please not me. Please! I hope this is a joke. I'm not going to have to sit next to some bubbly, bright-eyed, loud-mouthed Aussie all the way to fucking Oz, am I?'

His missus parked herself in the seat opposite the aisle. I was already on Plan B, which entailed my waiting for takeoff and then making some excuse to get up and go to the back and crash out. It was quite simple and straightforward.

I smiled at him and closed my eyes. I could sense he wasn't finished talking by a long chalk and somehow I knew what was coming next. 'What do you do, mate?' he asked me. He was a real-life Crocodile Dundee, but without the cork hat and Bowie knife.

I grunted something back about playing in a band, as though I were ashamed of it, then I closed my eyes. I didn't want to appear ignorant but I needed sleep.

'Where you from, mate?' I couldn't shut him up. I assumed he must have been on holidays with his missus for a while and needed some male company.

'Wales.' I was just about to add that it was the place in the UK where Tom Jones came from.

Then he piped up, 'Really? Where in Wales?'

'Do you know Wales?' I looked at him.

'Of course. We were there before we came to the States. My missus is from Treorchy.'

I straightened up. 'You're joking me.'

He wasn't. We started chatting. When we were airborne, the stewardess came up and he shouted, 'Miss, give me a VB [Victoria Beer] and one for my new mate, Stuey.'

I went to protest, but then I thought, 'When in Rome …' That was all the encouragement I needed. Next thing, I was back on the sauce and we were laughing and joking as though we'd been mates since we were kids. It didn't take much to top up my alcohol level. He was into designing trucks and he gave me his business card. I couldn't believe it when the captain informed us we were about to land. I had been on a 12-hour flight, which should have been just the opportunity to catch up on some much-needed rest, and instead I had spent most of it sinking VBs as if they were going out of fashion with my new best mate and his wife. But that sums me up, I think. I love to make new friends and get to know people. I'm quite a friendly old soul at heart.

We got off in Oz and the couple and I were all hugging and kissing. I was half-cut yet again. The rest of the band looked all fresh and wondered what the hell was going on. Kelly stood there shaking his head, but to be fair, he was smiling.

## DEMONS AND COCKTAILS

While we were in Australia, I really wanted to go and see the grave of my hero, Bonnie Scott. By then Kelly and I had made up, and while the rest went to the beach, we trooped off in search of the resting place of the main man. It turned out to be a weird old day. First, we went to the wrong cemetery – not once, but twice. When eventually we found the grave, we stood there, heads hung low in respect. It was hard to explain how I felt, but it was quite emotional. We didn't say a word to each other. I was surprised how understated the grave was. I had expected something worthy of a rock star, but all there was at the time was a small plaque with the odd beer bottle lying around here and there.

I looked up and noticed a large parrot sitting on a tree limb staring at us. I had never seen a parrot in the wild before. The closest I had come to an exotic bird was a slightly off-colour pigeon walking about in Aberdare Park. 'Fucking hell, that's weird,' I thought. I knew Bonnie had a parrot tattoo on his arm and for a split second I thought the bird was some kind of sign that he had come to see us. I nudged Kelly. Shivers raced down my spine until I looked around and saw that there were fucking loads of them flying about! Shame. It could have been such a good story to tell people.

Kelly's and my friendship went through lots of ups and downs throughout our success. One minute we were the best of mates, the next we were ready to kill each other, and the tension of touring didn't help. On one occasion, I was flying alone to LA. I can't remember what he was mad at me for. Kelly and Richard had gone over early and had taken their girlfriends with them.

Nicola had just had Cian, so she couldn't come. I was flying upper class on Virgin. All the air hostesses knew us because we always used them, especially on the LA route.

I started chatting away to the girls. These girls were bloody gorgeous; they were the next best thing to top-drawer models. The band were due to play a few gigs and do a video shoot in the city, so I asked the girls if they fancied coming for a drink later that night. It was the time when they used to stay over for a few days between flights. I must have been drunk, because I think I told them that if they turned up, the drinks were on me. But I knew it would be worth every penny just to wind up Kelly and Richard.

I got to the hotel, checked in and phoned Simon to find out where they all were. I then contacted one of the stewardesses to inform her about the arrangements. I got to the bar and, as I expected, the atmosphere was a little frosty.

I said my quick hellos and went to sit with the boys from the crew. We were having a craic. I told Simon about the girls turning up. 'This'll be bloody great!' Suddenly a big white stretch limo pulled up and a dozen beautiful girls got out. Kelly's and Richard's faces dropped to the floor.

'Hey, ladies, over here.' I motioned to them. They all came over, hugging and kissing me. I looked across and could see Kelly and Richard trying to explain these beautiful creatures to their girlfriends.

About thirty minutes later, Kelly's missus went to the toilet and he came rushing over to me. 'What the fuck are you doing?'

'What?' I played dumb. I knew one of the hostesses had a thing for him.

'You know what! My missus is here. It's not funny.'

'Well, my wife ain't!' I snapped back. The rest of the crew were dying to laugh.

When Kelly's girlfriend came out, they soon drank up and left, which was fine by me. The rest of us had a great night with the girls.

But the crew and I had lots of great times like that. Unfortunately, life on the road is full of temptations and some of the nights weren't anywhere near as innocent as the one with the Virgin girls. Some were really bizarre, others downright sordid.

I probably shouldn't even be divulging the details of one of the biggest demons that gripped us, since it violates the code of the road, and I know it will most likely end up getting some of the crew and me in deep trouble with our families. But I think it's important for people to understand that there really is a dark downside behind the scenes of a rock band's world that can destroy the soul and lead to addictions that can eventually leave you penniless. Fortunately, we were strong enough to escape any long-lasting ill effects, but it did take its toll mentally on most of us.

One night I remember quite vividly was during one of the USA tours. It was really late and we were all jetlagged, which probably only magnified our inability to think rationally. We locked the door and pulled the curtains in a desperate attempt to hide our indiscretions. One of the crew had rolled a few joints and passed them around. We kicked off our shoes and I clicked on the TV. The most gorgeous piece of ... cutlery you have ever seen was on sale: 'Buy today at the low price of $19.99.' We couldn't bring ourselves to look away, because we had sold our soul to the Shopping Channel devil. It was a real low point for all of us, even too painful to talk about today.

We stayed up all night, giggling and munching on snacks. It became our addiction. Looking back now, we probably should have booked ourselves into rehab for shopaholics.

The conversation in the room was hilarious.

'Order it, butt,' Simon would say. 'Go on, it's just what you need.'

I would study the set of kitchen knives and wonder what my missus would say.

'She'll love them.' Simon knew how to pull my trigger.

'I'm not sure. We've already got a set.'

But the guy on the TV could somehow sense my indecision and would try to entice me by adding extras. 'By the way, that's not all. We would also like to give you … a … free …'

We would watch with bated breath. Then they would cut to a commercial. I hate American TV. It's full of adverts, every five minutes. It takes nearly three hours to watch a 90-minute film. Anyway, during the adverts we would take bets on what the freebie was going to be. That was the best time, completely bonkers.

'What will it be?' I found myself asking.

'Spoons,' someone would pipe up.

'Forks.'

'A rubber shark.'

Laughter would fill the room. The dope had kicked in.

'What the fuck would they be offering a rubber shark with a set of fucking kitchen knives for?' I was serious.

'Maybe they had a job lot.'

I would piss myself laughing. Whoever was in the next room

must have been wondering what the hell was going on. So instead of going out on Sunset Strip picking up hookers or looking to score drugs like most rock stars and their roadies, I was in a room with my mates buying stuff I didn't need from a weird guy on TV with teeth you could see from the moon.

In the morning, I used to wake up and think, 'Oh, fuck, what did I buy last night? Kitchen knives, wineglasses, decanter, cuddly bear…' My mind was like the conveyor belt on *The Generation Game*. I needed to buy suitcases just to get the stuff back home. But it was a great way to unwind for a couple of hours until the madness of the day job started up again. And it was far better than getting addicted to the religious programmes that aired on Sunday mornings. Now that's what I would call seriously demented stuff.

Even today I still take a quick peep at the shopping channels when no one's around. Maybe I should see if there's an equivalent to an AA meeting just to get me off my weird addiction.


The attention we were getting from beautiful girls, the press and celebrities was starting to make us quite conceited and cocky. I remember the tour where we played all the big venues in major cities across Europe. It was hard work. On the last leg of the tour, we played 3 sell-out shows in Manchester to 18,000 people per night. On the second night, we had been told that David Beckham and some of the Manchester United boys were coming and they wanted to meet us afterwards.

So, after the gig, we were in the dressing room when a guy called John stuck his head around the door. 'Hey boys, I have someone here to meet you.'

'Okay, bring him in.'

## WHOLE LOTTA TOURING

It got to the point where playing stadiums and then meeting 'important' stars was run-of-the-mill; we just started to take it all in our stride. We weren't in awe of anyone any more – well, not as much as we used to be, anyway. We considered ourselves to be the main men around at the time; the stars the other stars were coming out to see. We were on the radio, in the charts, in the papers, on the billboards, everywhere. We had got to the point where we didn't need to blow smoke up anyone's arse any more.

So in strolled David Beckham, looking a million dollars. We all just sat there, not even an eyebrow raised. Blasé as fuck. I was in the corner, towel around me, eating Doritos. How cool was I? They weren't even Wotsits or Walker's cheese-and-onion crisps, just an average pack of cheesy Doritos. It was all laidback shit. Kelly was lying on a settee reading a paper, he didn't give a fuck. 'Alright, butt,' he said to the most famous footballer in the world, as if he were a paperboy or something. How mad is that? We were in the same room as one of the biggest sports stars on the planet and I was more concerned with going home in a few days' time.

Richard as usual didn't say a word, just nodded. Beckham told us he loved the show.

I did make an effort and I asked him who he was with.

'What?' he was quite shy.

'Are you by yourself?'

'No, I'm with Gary Neville. He's outside.'

I'm a massive Liverpool fan and the name Gary Neville is like waving a red rag to a bull. I jumped up and headed for the door. I opened it and saw him just wandering around. 'Get in here, you Manchester United twat,' I muttered.

He looked shocked and laughed nervously. I was only messing about with him and went to grab him in a headlock.

We talked for a while. I was meeting the infamous Mickey Thomas for drinks after the show. Now Mickey must have been one of the most colourful players, both on and off the field, who ever kicked a ball. He had just been released from prison for forgery. I asked David and Gary if they wanted to come for a drink with us to some club in town. Beckham said he would love to, but he knew that if the press caught him drinking even water, they would snap a photo of him and it would be all over the papers the next day and his manager, Alex Ferguson, would rip a strip off him. That must have been a tough life. Thank God I wasn't a footballer.

When I met up with Mickey later that night, I mentioned that I had been talking to Beckham. He joked that he had made as much money as Beckham did per week – until the police found the printing press. I had a great laugh with him and I'll never forget the time he bought the first round by the bar. Instead of opening his wallet like normal people, he reached down and pulled the money out of his sock. I looked at him. He whispered, 'Never trust these Manchester bastards.'

'Stuart is a happy-go-lucky character. He reminds me a bit of myself. He's got a great personality, so much energy, always willing to give up his time to talk and get to know people. I felt for him when he left the band; it was a great shame to have something so wonderful taken away from him. I felt sad because I thought the band were one big family who would get over their differences and just keep going, but I know he'll get over it and survive.

'He is a legend to me and I love him to death.'

**Mickey Thomas, ex-footballer for Wrexham, Manchester United and Wales**

# CHAPTER 7

# ASDA PRICE

Around the time of making our third album, *Just Enough Education to Perform*, and still continuing to tour, I found myself going through some dramatic changes within my work and personal life. First, and unbelievably, I embarked on a TV career as a chat-show host, discovered the hidden pleasures of cocaine, and not long afterwards, fell head over heels in lust with another woman.

Although I'm often told I have a good face for radio, I was offered the opportunity to host a show on BBC called *Cable TV* in 2002. It started with discussions between John and me about taking advantage of my strong voice and bubbly personality to host a Welsh chat show or rock programme. We talked about it with a few people at the Pop Factory, the music and media complex in Porth, Rhondda, who liked the concept and recommended that we pitch it to the BBC. And, just like that, my TV career began. So there I was, not only drummer with the top band of the moment in the UK, but also about to embark on a career to become the Welsh Parkinson. Who the hell would have bloody thought it?

I was excited, but really, really nervous. We started to put some names together for the show. I called in a favour from some of the stars that I had met down the years, people like Sir Tom, Howard Marks, Rhys Ifans, Neil Morrissey, Rob Brydon....All in all, I did 2 series with 6 episodes in each.

I also went on to do a spin-off show called *Cable Connect*, in which I spent a day in the life of a star. It was me just having a load of fun with some nice people. I used to travel around in a big yellow taxi, interviewing famous people. I loved that show and the format; it was more laidback. *Cable TV* was nerve-racking as hell, but *Cable Connect* really suited me down to the ground. I could just relax, be myself and enjoy the odd perk along the way.

I remember doing one episode with the lovely Katherine Jenkins. I travelled around with her on a typical day in her life. We started off in London in the Harrods department store with the launch of her new album. After a few hours of her signing autographs, we jumped in the car and headed down to her old school at Neath Abbey Hall in Wales, where she gave out awards to some of the pupils. We finished about ten o'clock that night and then I went home, unfortunately all alone.

Another time I went to London to spend the day with Rhys Ifans. He was doing a one-man show, in which he played five different parts during his performance. He was absolutely fantastic. It was so good I felt like crying at the end. I don't think we realise just how great an actor he is. When he was taking his bow on stage, he looked across at me and winked, gesturing for us to go for a pint. So after the show we had a couple of beers and then went driving around the West End. He told me I had the loudest laugh he had ever heard in the theatre.

At the end of the interview I asked him where he thought he would be in ten years' time. He gave me his wicked look; he's got to be the wickedest, but nicest guy in show business. 'Where I see myself in ten years' time, Stuart my boy, is me and you on a beach in Thailand, naked with two Thai boys greased and ready for action.' The picture he painted in my mind was quite disturbing. Pity we had to cut his reply out of the episode.

I met some really interesting stars during that opportunity: Ainsley Harriott, Neil and Christine Hamilton, Noddy Holder the vocalist and guitarist for Slade, Keith Chegwin, and many more. Uri Geller came on and gave me a signed spoon that he had personally bent just for me. What a conversation piece! When people went to Adam Duritz's house, he would proudly boast that it once belonged to David Niven. When people came to visit me, the only thing I could do was pull out a rather strange-looking bent spoon from the drawer and ask them to try and guess who gave it to me. Not surprisingly, they would normally get the answer without much help.

The TV stuff was daunting to start with. When I see clips of the programme now, I realise I was stiff as a board in the first couple of shows. I was like a robot, a stuttering R2D2. It was the scariest thing I have ever done. It's easy to go on stage and bash drums in front of thousands of people with your mates; it's easy when you're lost in the band, 'all for one and one for all'. I was always full of confidence when I was seated at my drums, but television was a different matter altogether. I was on my own and had to remember what I wanted to say to people, or look like an idiot. I had to remember to read the autocue, check the cue cards and listen to what the producer and the guests were saying, all at the same time. It was a nightmare, especially for someone with my attention span, but it made me appreciate just how good guys like Michael Parkinson, Terry Wogan and Jonathan Ross really are. They make it look so easy. It is a gift that not many people possess.

I did get better as I progressed through the episodes, although there are probably lots of people who would disagree. I think I would piss the show now, do it standing on my hair. I recall the barrage of Welsh Valleys humour that came out to greet me when I went back to my local for a beer, just like in the good ol' days. 'Stu, you should stick to playing drums, and you're crap at that.' Or, 'I've seen parking meters with more personality than you.'

I know the show was a bit of what some would call 'car crash' TV to start with, especially when Howard Marks came on. He was so stoned he could hardly speak. I whispered to him, 'C'mon, Howie, you gotta help me out, man, you gotta answer some questions.'

But the show had its moments. One funny story concerns the episode when I interviewed the great Tom Jones. Comedy is all about timing and I always wanted to be that funny comedy type of guy. We were in the studio and it was just before we were about to start recording. It was absolutely sweltering in the Pop Factory in Porth. I mean, a sweat-dripping-off-your-back type of heat. I was a bag of nerves about interviewing the larger-than-life legend to start with, even though I knew him quite well. And it was really uncomfortable under the lights – I was sweating with all the make-up on.

It was all quiet and we were ready to begin recording.

'Ladies and gentlemen,' I said. 'Please put your hands together for Mr Tom Jones.'

Just at that moment, high up in the viewing gallery, which must have been unbearably hot, a woman fainted. And, as quick as a flash, I turned to Tom and said, 'You still haven't lost it, Tom.' He burst out laughing and thankfully it set the tone for the rest of the interview.

One of the best things he told me during our conversation was about the time he was playing in one of the major hotels in Las Vegas. After a while he began to notice that everything was coming back from the laundry except his underwear. It became obvious that someone in the launderette was making a fast buck selling Tom Jones's underwear. The story made me picture underwear thieves selling them on a street corner: 'Tom Jones's underwear for sales. Fifty bucks a pair, or three for a hundred.'

He said he was flattered at first but soon got sick and tired of buying new ones, so he started washing his own briefs by wearing them in the shower after the gig and then hanging them up to dry in his room. You can take the Tom out of Wales, but you can't take Wales out of the Tom.

I had a great rapport with Tom, both on and off the camera, and we became good mates after the show. Funnily enough, some people still joke today that I am really his love child. One night when I was drunk, I started quizzing him about how he could be with so many women over the years and have the reputation of a world-class womaniser, yet manage to keep his wife. I think I said something like, 'I bet it's because your wife's got a good-looking gardener called Ramone.' I was only joking.

I could see the wheels in his mind start turning. After a while he turned to me and said, 'He *is* a good-looking bloke.' I think he was quite miffed about it, which made me smile. The pot calling the kettle black or what?

Tom is great at storytelling. The tales he's told me about meeting Richard Burton and Elvis and a host of others are just unbelievable. Like the night Frank Sinatra had a restaurant closed down completely for the evening, just so he and Tom could have a good meal and a few drinks without people watching them.

Sometime later, we were asked by Tom's son, who is his manager, if we fancied appearing on the Jools Holland's New Year's Eve show with Tom. John phoned to tell us the news. 'Tom's doing *Hootenanny* with Jools and was wondering if you fancied going down for a bit of a knees-up.' That was the type of informal relationship we had with him at the time.

Only Kelly and I went. We were in London, anyway. I think Richard was away somewhere else at the time.

It was a great night. We had a few beers and ended up singing 'Hi Ho Silver Lining' with the 'voice'. I was steaming, dancing my tits off like a fool.

After the programme there was a bit of a party backstage. Tom, as usual, was holding court, telling his tales of days gone by. There was Kelly, a couple of girls, Chrissie Hynde from the Pretenders, Jools and Mark Lamarr, from the TV show *Never Mind the Buzzcocks*, and myself.

To be honest, I didn't particularly like Mark Lamarr. To put it mildly, I always thought he was an unfunny, sarcastic prick. The party was going well. Everyone was laughing and enjoying Tom's stories. Lamarr kept chipping in with this and that, trying to be funny. It was soon obvious that others didn't like him, either. People round the table were straining to smile at his jokes and his cute little remarks. I tried to just ignore him. Anyway, he said something about Wales and, messing about, I said, 'Why don't you fuck off, you nifty-fifty bin man?' It was what Bob Mortimer and Vic Reeves used to call him on their show.

He turned and replied, 'Who are you talking to, you Welsh cunt?'

There was silence. Everyone looked down at the table. It was really awkward. Tom looked at me, his face serious. He said slowly, 'Stu, are you going to knock him out, or am I?'

I was fuming myself. 'Don't worry, Tom, I'll sort it.' I turned to Lamarr. 'Okay, outside.'

He turned to Tom. 'Look, Tom, I'm sorry, sorry. I didn't mean anything.'

Tom sipped his champagne and grunted at him. 'You better move, sonny.' He was like a Clint Eastwood in *Dirty Harry*, but a big Welsh version: Tom Eastwood in *Slightly Unwashed Dai*.

Jools was trying to cool the situation down. I have never really been what you would call a fighter, or in fact a lover, or some might say a drummer either, but I was bouncing so high I wanted to kick his greased-up quiff off his shoulders. We went out into the corridor. After a couple of sharp words I told him he was spoiling everyone's night and that he should fuck off. He went to say something, but just looked at me and walked out. I went back in and joined the party. Tom winked at me as though I were, after all, the long-lost seed of his overactive loins.

Another earlier occasion, we had performed with Tom at the Brit Awards singing 'Mama Told Me Not to Come'. That was the night, if I remember correctly, Andrea Corr, the Irish singer and actress, was all over Kelly like a rash. What a jammy, good-looking, talented little bastard he was at times!

I was standing by the bar with Mr Jones, the last of the big-time drinkers. I was on the beer, he was on the shampoo. I was leaning on the bar when this guy walked over to us. I was sure I recognised him, but couldn't make out where from.

He tapped Tom on the shoulder. 'Tom, I would just like to tell you what a big influence you've been on my career and my life. I've always loved your vocals, love the way you're still producing great music.'

The guy was really blowing smoke up Tom's arse. There was something about him. He looked so familiar. I then realised it was Ian Gillian from Deep Purple. How the hell could I not have known who he was? I should have been horsewhipped and dragged through my village with no clothes on for not realising it straight off.

I ran over to Julian, who was on camera duty that night, and told him to bring his gear with him. We rushed back over. I waited respectfully for their conversation to die down. He was still brown-nosing Tom.

'Mr Gillian, do you mind if I have a picture with you, please?' I was as polite as I could be.

He screwed up his face and basically told me, in no uncertain terms, to fuck off. I was shocked, speechless. I went to skulk off into the shadows. Then Tom stepped in. 'What did you say?' he asked him.

Gillian hadn't clicked I was with Tom. He rolled his eyes as if I was nobody. 'I haven't got time.'

Tom quietly grunted, 'Look, if the boy wants a picture, the boy will have a picture.'

I was disappointed at the guy's attitude and told Tom it was alright and I didn't want one now. But I could see Tom's face getting red. 'You will have one.' He turned to Julian. 'You, take the fucking picture.'

It was quite awkward as I stood silently next to the Deep Purple singer to have a photograph, which by that time I didn't really want. When it was over, I said something like, 'Cheers, butt.'

Tom tapped Ian on the shoulder and said straight out, 'Now you can fuck off.'

I looked at Julian; he looked at me. We were both too scared to glance in Ian's direction. Inside I was chuffed as he walked away. Tom necked his drink and ordered another. I couldn't believe *the* Tom Jones had stuck up for me over *the* Ian Gillian from Deep Purple.


The TV shows were positive things in my life at that time. I got to meet some really great people and expand my horizons. Unfortunately, there were also drugs and other temptations that I just couldn't pass up.

I'm not sure if I'm ashamed to tell anyone I took drugs or not. I know in years to come, my son will probably read this and may be shocked or embarrassed at some of the choices I've made along the way. I'm not condoning what I did, but don't forget that I was a rock star in a rock'n'roll world, and that's what rock stars do: dabble in illegal substances. Besides, what else was a weird-looking bastard from a small village, who suddenly found himself flying first-class around the world, playing in front of thousands of adoring fans and hosting his own TV show, supposed to do? Become a nun or sit in his room and order knives from the Shopping Channel?

The only problem is that I don't do anything in moderation and so, when I finally got on the road to Drugtown, it was full on, pedal to the metal, no second thoughts of slowing down and looking at the scenery. I had the wind in my hair and the powder up my nose and that was all the fuel I required to get me to wherever I needed to go, as fast as I needed to get there.

I first began doing what some would call 'serious drugs' not with the band, as one might think, but when I started presenting *Cable TV*. One day a cameraman on the set came over and said, 'Hey, Stu, fancy some charlie?' His brother was a dealer and was looking to offload some gear.

Of course, I wasn't stupid and naïve enough not to know what charlie was. I was a man of the world; I'd seen *Twin Town* loads of times. 'Charlie, Peruvian marching powder, fucking snow!' I had seen people in the business take it, but I had never done it before myself. Not saying I was an angel; I had always smoked a little weed and of course there was the PR spray incident in my old school days, but this was a new sensation for me, and, sadly, a sensation that I grew to like way too much. It was amazing and made me feel great. It was also unfortunate that the stuff I was offered was cheap, so I could buy as much as I wanted. It was only 120 big ones for 7g. In London at the same time it was selling at £55 for 1g.

'Asda prices,' the cameraman used to mutter to me and tap the back pocket of his jeans, as they do in the Asda ads. 'Cable, these are fucking Asda prices! I bet you Lidl doesn't do it cheaper than that.' And he was right. It was a bargain and such a good deal that, as soon as I started to sample it, I didn't want to stop. My inner demons had awoken and wanted to party.

By the release of our fourth album, *You Gotta Go There to Come Back*, some of the crew and I were already heavily into our drugs. We even came up with a piss-take name for the album, *You Gotta Go There to Get Gak*, which was slang for cocaine. I know it was childish but we thought it was hilarious.

I recall when, during the launch party in a posh part of London, two of the craziest Welsh lunatics you are ever likely to meet turned up: Rhys Ifans and Howard Marks. I was already on top form and enjoying myself by then.

After a bit, Howard tugged my arm and asked if I fancied a nice little line. He didn't have to ask twice. 'Fucking great, How!' I replied and we headed to the toilet. As we walked through the crowd of people, for some unknown reason I asked him, 'Is it any good, How?' As soon as I said it, I shook my head. Who did I think I was talking to, some hoodie I'd just met in a nightclub? Some pimp hiding in an alleyway? I couldn't believe I had just asked 'the Man' the most stupid question on earth. This was the man who had a first-class honours degree in supplying drugs. The one-time most-wanted drug baron on the planet, *the* Howard fucking Marks of the drug world, and I had asked him if his stuff was any good. If he wasn't such a lovely bloke, he would have had his mates, the Outlaws, kneecap me or shoot me for being so fucking dim. Instead he stopped and looked at me. He shrugged his shoulders, before replying in his thick, Welsh accent: 'Is it any good?' He chuckled to himself and walked on. I followed him like a puppy dog to the bog.

When we got to the restroom, there was a black guy over by the sinks handing out all the samples of aftershave and other assorted smellies.

'We can't go in the cubicle together with him there,' I whispered nervously, looking across at him.

'Leave it to me,' he whispered.

He walked up to the attendant, a 20-quid note in his hand. 'What's your name, fellow?' he asked the man, who was staring at the note as if it were a watch being swung by a hypnotist. The guy told him his name and grinned as Howard placed the money in his top pocket. 'See my mate over there?' He pointed to me. I smiled like a complete arse and held my thumb up. 'Well, I'm going to take him into the bog and I'm going to give him the best blowjob he's ever had. But it must be our secret, all undercover but his underwear. Alright?' I stopped smiling and put my thumb down.

'Shit!' I thought. Had I heard Howard correctly when he'd asked me in the bar if I wanted some charlie? Or did he actually ask me if I fancied a blowjob? I started to panic a little. It had been noisy in the club and I knew he had spent 7 long years in a maximum-security prison in the States.

The black guy winked and went about his business. He didn't care a fuck; he had probably made more money in that one go than he had made all night. We locked the door behind us and the king of dope gave me the best blowjob I ever had. No, only messing. We cut up some lines and I sampled some of the finest coke I have ever had. The funny thing was that, later in the night, Howard realised he had lost the bag of coke.

'Where's the gear?' he asked.

'You had it,' I replied.

'Oh, no.'

We both rushed to the bog and unbelievably it was still there on top of the china pan. We decided it would be a shame not to sample a little more. I wonder if the aftershave guy thought we were going in for a second helping of head.

I never forget that night, and every time I meet up with the former drug lord we always have a laugh about it. Howard is one cool mother and a truly interesting and super-intelligent gentleman. It's a pity the government, or whoever, hasn't made use of what the guy has to offer.

When we went on tour, coke was never far behind for me and some of the road crew. I never did drugs before a show, but once it was over I turned into some kind of coke-taking zombie. I wouldn't rest until I had my fill. It was party time and a white Christmas, all rolled into one.

We once played the Montrose Music Festival. At that stage we used to travel around in two buses, one for us and the other for the crew. I was on our bus. Kelly was preparing to put on another one of his favourite DVDs. I had seen it a million times; I was bored. I had received a text from the boys to say that they had just scored some good stuff, so I made some excuse and went to change coaches.

'Where are you going?' Kelly piped up. Before I had a chance to reply, he added, 'Oh, charlie, is it?'

'Could be, Kel. Each to their own. You like your films, I like something a little more exciting.' I left and joined the crew.

But that was me. I was always the type of person who arrived at a party first, and if I didn't end up too wasted, I was one of the last to leave. And the drugs had made me thirstier and crazier than ever.

All drugs are harmful, but shit like cocaine takes its toll on a person. It changes your body, your personality, everything about you. It made me act selfishly towards people I really shouldn't have been selfish to.

I don't believe my drug-taking was the main reason, but it did have some influence over the band's and my decision to go our separate ways. The other two never took the stuff. Richard smoked a little weed; Kelly talked about taking coke (that was the rock star in him trying to get out), but I never saw him actually ever do it. It put me on a different level from them. In the early days everything was okay and quite simple. We would get drunk together and sometimes we would smoke a little blow, but the coke had split us up. We went from a tight-knit rock band, who were the best of friends, to the two musketeers against the hyperactive junkie clown. Sounds like a title for a bad B-movie.

The more we started to drift apart, the more I rebelled and went my own way. Looking back now, I know I was a pain in the arse. I can be a pain in the arse without the influence of drugs, so I can only imagine what it was like to be around me when I was high. During the recording of the *JEEP* album (*Just Enough Energy to Perform*), I developed a red rash around my lower back. I found out later it was a trait of cocaine abuse. We were in the studio and I spent most of the time scratching like a dog covered in flies. It got so bad I started bleeding. It was getting on my nerves, and everyone else's as well. You could cut the tension with a kitchen knife.

I never took anything stronger than coke, and I know in most people's eyes that's bad enough, but there was no heroin or horse tranquillisers, or any other shit like that. I could never understand how someone could stick a needle in their arm and inject God knows what into their veins. It was just a case of good old-fashioned cocaine for me when I needed to lift myself up.

But eventually it took over my life. I started to find it a hassle to hold a conversation with normal people. And that, as people who really know me will tell you, is not the real me. I love to talk to anyone at any time about anything. As time marched on, I found that this supposedly sociably accepted drug caused me to become highly unsociable for long periods of time. Even my shopping-channel experiences with the crew weren't the same when there was a bowl of the white powder on the coffee table. All the innocence of our childish games had disappeared.

I knew it was changing me, but I was having too much of a good time to give it all up. We were camped out in the studio at a place called Hook End Manor in Oxfordshire, which was at one time the home of Dave Gilmour from Pink Floyd. The place was brilliant, a huge mansion surrounded by 14 acres of lush land. Making our latest album wasn't going well and work was quite stressful. The cracks in the band were already starting to appear. Kelly was very serious and trying hard to make the perfect album. Richard was his normal laid-back self, and I was bursting with energy, some of it natural, some chemically induced.

There was a girl there and we got on really well. To protect the innocent I am not going to say who she was. One day while I was busy in the studio, I packed her off and sent her all the way down to Wales to see my mate, just to pick up some charlie for us. I think it was about 8g of the stuff. Looking back now, I know there's no way I should have sent the girl to do my dirty work, but I needed it. I couldn't wait until we'd finished the recording sessions to get off my head.

When she got back, we proceeded to do the lot in, in under two days. We were high as kites, as well as plastered from the beer and shorts. On the second night, she decided she'd had enough and went up to bed. I, like the fool on the hill, carried on for a while longer. I had powder and a half bottle of Scotch to finish. When I finally retired myself, I thought I'd check to make sure she was alright. I knocked, but there was no answer. The bedroom door was unlocked. I entered and found her on the floor of the bathroom, in the nude, shaking. I shat myself. It was like the scene out of *Pulp Fiction*.

I didn't know what to do. I raced back and forth, from room to room. I wanted to scream for help, but at the same time I really didn't want Kelly and Richard to barge in and see what I had caused. She was still shaking violently. I held her tight, tears rolling down my face. I thought she was going to die, but luckily she rapidly cooled down and stopped trembling. She opened her eyes. I didn't know if I should laugh or cry. I put her into bed and unbelievably went downstairs to get a drink to calm my nerves.

Later that night, I lay in bed and vowed never to touch the stuff again. You might have thought that would have been my wake-up call, but it wasn't. I'm just not wired like that. Three days later, someone offered me a quick pick-me-up. Without thinking twice, I accepted it and leapt back on the train at full speed.

As if the cocaine wasn't bad enough, I became even more addicted to another drug that had nothing to do with manmade chemicals at all. It was during the *JEEP* stage of our lives. The band had been asked to make the presentations at the *Kerrang!* Awards for the best live band. We had won it two years on the trot, and although it would have been nice to have received it for the third time, we were honoured that they had asked us to present.

I had fond memories of reading the *Kerrang!* magazine when I was growing up. As far as I was concerned it was the *pièce de résistance* of the major music papers; it was our bible in Cwmaman. The first-ever issue had Angus Young on the front cover; I still have a copy in the attic in my mother's house. I never thought in a billion years that one day my group would be written about in my favourite magazine, let alone receive its prestigious awards.

On the night of the ceremony I walked up onto the stage and saw this girl standing on the sidelines. I thought she was absolutely gorgeous. I walked past her and rather bravely flicked her hair and grinned. She smiled back at me. I could feel my knees going weak.

After all the formal stuff, I made some excuse to go and talk to her. Her name was Lisa Rogers and she was a presenter on Channel 4 and E4. We clicked immediately. It was like two light bulbs coming on at the same time. We ended up talking, and talking, and talking for the reminder of the night. She was so easy to communicate with. Nothing happened between us, but the next day I felt as if like I were floating on air as I journeyed back home on the train. Something inside of me had been awakened. Halfway home she texted me to say she really enjoyed my company and that she would like to see me again if I was ever up that way. I'm ashamed to say I felt a bit guilty, because I hadn't told her I was married at first. She had made some comment about me being single, and I didn't tell her I wasn't. I didn't exactly lie, but I wanted her to want me. By the time I told her the truth it was too late and we'd fallen for each other. She was my new drug, and I didn't care how wrong it was, I simply couldn't get enough of her.

I couldn't wait to get back up to London. I made any excuse I could to go and see her. We met about two weeks later for dinner and that was that. I knew straightaway she was the one for me. To the outside world it must have seemed like I had changed overnight.

Nicola sensed something was up with me. Women have a knack of knowing things like that. And, to be fair, I was horrible to her. I was a prick and must have been a nightmare to live with. I would start fights on purpose so I could get away. Some nights the guilt of what I was doing used to rip me open inside. I was spilt in two: one side of me was alive and happy, the other half miserable and riddled with remorse. My moods bounced around and changed minute by minute. But in the end I felt really happy with Lisa, quite content with what we had, and what I pictured for the future.

It was all my doing. My entire life and outlook altered. I was not only hooked on drugs, but found myself addicted to another woman. I'm not going to say that what I did was right; I'm not going to blame it on the lifestyle I was living. It can happen to anyone. People fall in love all the time. I'd been with Nicola for a long time. Kelly and Richard had packed up and left their old girlfriends for the bright lights of London with all its temptations a long time before. Maybe it was their way of getting the inevitable out of their systems before they got in too deep.

Perhaps they knew something like this would happen to them if they had stayed. But I couldn't help it. I just found Lisa very sexy to be with. She was a bundle of energy; we laughed all the time. The chemistry between us was second to none. She was a good kid, very funny, has a great sense of humour and is extremely intelligent. One thing I like in a woman is intelligence, and she oozed it. And in return I gave her a rock'n'roll lifestyle, which for the most part she loved.

I spent as much time as possible with her. I took her on all of the trips with the band and we became inseparable. I think she loved being with me as well. And she put her life on hold for me. For the next year she didn't take any work; she wanted to come with me wherever we went.

The others in the band hated the situation. I think Kelly was pissed off because he thought he could pull her. She was a good-looking girl – stunning, in fact. She made people's heads turn when we walked into a room. He hated it because he didn't like the fact that his butty, the fat drummer with the big hair from Cwmaman, had pulled someone so absolutely stonking. He could pull women in abundance: he was good-looking, talented, dark and mysterious, and he could have had any woman he wanted, except for my Lisa. She was mine.

It's funny how obsessed I became. I used to sit on the stage on my big drum riser, looking out on thousands and thousands of fans. I used to see her on the side of the stage. And, while I was performing, half of me was watching her, making sure no guy was making a hit on her. If I saw a guy walk within two metres of her, I wanted to get off my kit and beat him to death with my sticks. I would spend half the gig watching her instead of enjoying the best thing in the world. I was crazy, stupid. I was the one on stage, with girls looking up at us, and I didn't care. She was the one I wanted.

Lisa bought me one of the best presents I have ever had. She commissioned a painter in London to paint a portrait of Bonnie Scott for my 30th birthday. God knows how much it must have cost her. I have it in the hallway of my new house, but I haven't got around to hanging it up yet – it's still just leaning against the wall. One day …

Lisa and I were having a ball and enjoying the good life together, but, as usual, I went and fucked it up. I got too sentimental, too nostalgic about it all, and the inevitable break-up was hard to take. But I'll discuss that later.

For some bizarre and twisted reason everyone wants to know what my favourite Stereophonics songs are. Okay, here we go …

My number-one 'Phonics song of all time is, of course, **'Dakota'**. No, fuck off! I'd rather eat my own toenails.

**'Same Size Feet'** – I love the story behind it. It's about a man and a woman having a secret love affair but then the man goes missing. His lover is not sure where he's gone. She thinks the worst when they find a body in the lake with the same size feet as his. It still makes me wonder when I listen to it, even today, if he really died or just got bored and moved on to someone new, or back to his wife. I guess I'll never know.

'**Plastic California**' – I remember Kelly writing it after the first time we went to LA. Someone said it looked like Blackpool Pleasure Beach, but more out of date. It always reminded me of a Tragically Hip type of song.

'**Rooftop**' – I used to love to play it live. The whole melody line, the build-up at the end; I love it. And of course my old mate Glen played harmonica on it.

'**I Stopped to Fill My Car Up**' – Kelly had learnt only 4 chords on a piano and came up with the song. It was an old shaggy-dog kind of story, which he somehow made sound so creepy and real. Not many bands would have even attempted to do something like that, never mind pull it off.

'**Check My Eyelids for Holes**' – it was a saying in Cwmaman. I remember going camping in my teens and someone would always say it when they fell asleep. What are you doing? Nothing – just checking my eyelids for holes. (I wonder who first came up with that. How clever!) It was also one of the first songs we wrote together in the early days.

## CHAPTER 8

# IT'S ONLY SHEPHERD'S PIE
# (BUT I LIKE IT)

**D**uring the height of our fame, we were really privileged to support some of the biggest bands on the planet. We got to tour around with some of the biggest, and on occasion the maddest, names in the world of rock: U2, Aerosmith, Bon Jovi and many more. It was a fantastic experience getting to know those guys and to witness first hand all their quirks, routines and often their little temper tantrums. But it was nothing compared to the time when we supported the godfathers of rock'n'roll, the Rolling Stones, in Europe. Now *that* was the mother of all experiences, Volume 69!

We were with them in France and we had just finished our set in Marseille. Kelly's voice was electric. To be honest, he could hold his own with the best of them.

After the gig I was starving. I rarely eat before concerts, so after the last note is played and we're trooping off stage, I'm usually looking for something to tuck into. And, fuck me, the Stones had the most extravagant after-show banquet I had ever seen. There were six-foot ice sculptures lining the tables, candles flickering around the room and an army of waitresses standing around like scared rabbits caught in headlights. Food of every description was laid out as far as the eye could see. It made me laugh to think back to some of our early gigs in Wales, where we were lucky to get a flagon of White Lightning cider, three Pot Noodles and a paper plate of paste sandwiches. And now, here we were, sitting at the top table eating from the hands of ultimate rock gods.

I strolled through the line of grub: salmon, caviar, truffles and loads of different finger-food nibbles. There was enough food to feed a Third World country for a bloody month. It was exactly like one of those posh wedding receptions you see in *Hello!* magazine.

I had to rub my eyes twice to make sure I wasn't dreaming when I saw a big, fuck-off baking tray of shepherd's pie at the edge of the massive table in between the roasted pig's head and the gigantic plate of sushi.

'Kelly, Kelly, there's shepherd's pie!' I said, like an excited ten-year-old at Christmas.

'Whatever,' came the reply, as he nibbled on a chicken satay and walked off.

Undeterred, I went for it, whacking several hefty spoonfuls onto my plate. I loved shepherd's pie; it was my favourite dish. I would eat it morning, noon and night, and twice on Christmas Day if I could.

Back in the dressing room, I sat in the corner with my top off, talking with the guys from the crew and having a laugh, when there was a knock at the door. It was Ronnie Wood. We had met

Ronnie a few times in the past, at various events we played at. He was a mate of ours and a good ambassador for the band. He really liked us.

'Hi, boys. Mick would like to meet you.'

Our faces froze as the ageing lead singer ambled in. I wasn't sure if I should stand, curtsy or clap. He was royalty with a capital R. I half expected a fanfare of trumpets to announce his arrival and several corgi dogs to follow him in; I felt naked in his presence. I searched about for my top. Shit! It was at the other end of the room. I tried to cover myself up.

The dressing room went silent. Mick introduced himself. 'I loved the show, boys. Glad to have you on board.'

He turned to me and nodded in an 'I know something about you' sort of way, and then spoke in his distinctive English accent. 'Hey Stuart, I know what you like to drink.'

Everyone stared at me as if I was some kind of freak in a travelling circus. I nearly spat a mouthful of minced meat over the table. How the hell did the most famous singer in the world know what I liked to drink? I looked at Kelly, who was standing behind Mick. He just shrugged. I racked my brains for some kind of clue.

A five-star rock god was telling me that he knew what I liked to drink. Had I been out drinking with him in a past life? Could he tell what I liked by the way I played drums? Was he really Janice, the landlady from the Welsh Harp in Aberdare, on his day off? I was so confused.

'You don't know what I'm talking about, do you?' he snorted cruelly.

I shook my head.

**145**

'You like Guinness and Southern Comforts.'

'Bloody hell!' I thought. 'Not even my mother knows that.'

He grinned and continued: 'I saw you on Jools Holland's show.'

I breathed out. Mystery solved. We had been on Jools' show several weeks before talking about life on the road and our favourite tipples and all that rock-star sort of stuff.

I shook his hand. The Jaggerman then stopped in his tracks and the pleasantness suddenly left his face. 'Who's eating that?' he pointed to the half-eaten plate of shepherd's pie on the table, which was littered with cigarette butts and cans of beer.

I put my hand up like a schoolkid in class asking to go to the toilet.

He chuckled and made a face, rolling his eyes to the ceiling. 'Do you know the rules?'

'What rules?' I replied. I felt like the black guy in the boiler house in the film *Scum* before he got beaten up by Carling with a lead pipe.

'These fuckin' rules.' I imagined him hitting me straight across the face with his rock-hard reply. 'There are only two things you don't do when you tour with us.' He seemed to take pleasure in what he was about to say. Again, everyone stared at me and then back towards Mick. 'One' – he held his finger up – 'you don't play on the snooker table unless you've been asked.'

Later on that night I found out that Richard had turned to Kelly and muttered under his breath, 'What, a fuckin' *real* snooker table?'

'No,' Kelly whispered back sarcastically, 'a fuckin' jokin' one.'

Mick continued, 'And, secondly, you never, *ever*, take the shepherd's pie unless Keith's broken the crust first.'

Kelly and John, our manager, shot dagger eyes at me. I looked at them both in an 'I didn't fucking know there were two things we weren't supposed to do when you tour with the fucking Rolling Stones, and if I did I wouldn't think that eating fucking shepherd's pie would be top of the list' sort of way. To be honest, I wouldn't have thought playing snooker on a real portable table would be the other.

'Did you break the crust?' Mick asked smugly.

'Of course I broke the crust.' I wanted to answer him. 'How the hell could I have a plateful of the stuff without breaking the crust? Do I look like fuckin' Paul Daniels or that American guy who stood in a big glass cage in London?' Instead I nodded again.

Mick smiled; it was lined with childlike wickedness. He twirled on his heels and said jokingly, before heading out, 'Enjoy the show, boys. If there *will* be a show. I'm not sure if he'll go on after this.' At least I thought it was a joke.

Ronnie shook his head slowly and disappeared behind him.

There was silence in our dressing room yet again. 'What?' I looked at everyone.

'You better take it back and see if they can re-crust it,' John cried.

'Fuck off!' I held another spoonful near to my lips.

'Great idea.' Kelly jumped up to examine the remains on the plate.

A heated discussion followed concerning what should be done to rectify the situation. Although I thought I put up a reasonably good argument for just eating the bloody thing, I was outvoted three to one. So it was then left to me to make the long walk back to catering, carrying the half-eaten plate of food as if it were a bomb ready to explode.

## DEMONS AND COCKTAILS

As I strolled alone I began to wonder what would have happened if I hadn't owned up to the shepherd's-pie crime. Would they have brought in a detective to fingerprint everything? Might they have sealed all the doors until the evidence had come out the other end? And, more importantly, was it really that big a deal? I could picture the headlines in some of the national music press and our local paper:

*NME* – RICHARDS REFUSES TO GO ON STAGE AFTER SHEPHERD'S PIE CATASTROPHE … WORLD TOUR CANCELLED

**Q magazine** – KELLY DISTRAUGHT … LOCKS HIMSELF AWAY AND WRITES 45-MINUTE ACOUSTIC SONG ABOUT THE SHAMEFUL NIGHT … 'THE BARTENDER AND THE PIE THIEF'

*Aberdare Leader* (our local paper), front page – EXCLUSIVE: MABEL CABLE TELLS US HER SECRET RECIPE FOR HOW TO COOK THE PERFECT PIE FOR HER LITTLE BOY

*Aberdare Leader* again, page 5 – MAN FROM CWMAMAN SELLS TWO KIDS ON EBAY TO PAY FOR HIS BENYLIN HABIT

Luckily, when I got to catering I knew the waitress – she had worked with us on the U2 tour. She took it back and shook her head slowly and muttered, 'Don't you know the rules?'

**148**

'No!' I wanted to scream at her. 'And if you knew the bloody rules you should have put an out-of-bounds label on it, or surrounded the baking tray with barbed-wire fencing and posted an Alsatian dog next to it.' But I knew it wasn't her fault and instead I just shrugged and grinned.

She went to work on it and soon re-laid the potato topping and made it as good as new, even if it was a little thinner. Major world disaster averted. Later that night the Stones did go on stage, with Keith, and blew everyone away. They were brilliant.

The next day, it was Paris. A bigger gig held in the new spiritual home of French rugby, the Stade de France. We got there in the early afternoon to make sure we had a reasonably good sound check. The stadium was awesome. I looked out across the rows of empty terraces and imagined 80,000 Parisian supporters baying for Welsh blood as they watched their team on the battlefield. Hopefully, tonight the atmosphere would be a lot friendlier with 50,000 French men and women singing the chorus to 'Le Local Boy dans Le Photograph'.

After the sound check we relaxed in our dressing room, which was situated way up in the gods. We were going through the set for later that night, making some last-minute adjustments, when there was a knock on the door.

'I haven't touched the fuckin' shepherd's pie, honest,' I joked. Everyone laughed.

Richard opened the door and he rocked back on his heels. There, blocking out the doorway, were two of the biggest bouncers I had ever seen. I always thought the bouncers in the Black Lion in the centre of Aberdare were big, mean hombres, but these guys were in a different league. The smaller, stockier one looked half man and half fuckin' dumper truck, with a head the size of a Black and Decker lawnmower.

He pointed to me and Kelly and grunted, 'You've been summoned.'

Richard, who, to be fair, is one of the hardest men I know, even breathed out, then smirked and went back to tuning his bass guitar.

We followed the two gorillas for what seemed like several miles through the grey empty concrete corridors of the stadium. They didn't talk, just swaggered on, knuckles dragging on the floor.

The two man-beasts stopped and pointed to a door. I gulped hard before tiptoeing through it; I wanted to hold Kelly's hand. Behind the door was a curtain, the type you would find sparkling on a stage in some rundown workingmen's club. We walked through it and met with a room engulfed in thick smoke, with a full-size snooker table taking centre stage and an illuminated scoreboard on the wall. My mouth dropped open. It *was* a rundown workingmen's club.

'Fuckin' hell, Kel,' I muttered under my breath. 'They'll be doing the tote next.'

Ronnie greeted us with his usual enthusiasm and cheeky grin. 'Welcome to the snake pit, boys.' He was wearing white snooker referee's gloves and cleaning the balls on the table.

It always amazed me how bizarre our life had become. A week earlier I had been teaching my little boy how to swim the crawl in Aberdare baths and now here I was, standing in the bloody snake pit with two of the world's original rock'n'roll pirates.

Kelly nudged me. Then I saw the governor through the fag smoke, or fag-and-some-other-substance smoke actually. Keith was sitting in the corner, dressed in his usual attire. He nodded in our direction before continuing to slice off thin strips of dope from the biggest piece of hash I had ever seen. He took his time. I was fascinated by his precision and technique; it reminded me of Pauly in the film, *Goodfellas*, slicing up garlic in prison.

Ronnie poured us a double vodka and orange. It was midday, but they were already on the razz.

'This is the life,' I thought. 'I wish our old headmaster could see me now.'

'Cable!' I could picture him yelling across the class at me with his super-serious face on. 'You will never be anything in your life, boy.'

I floated off into my imagination. 'Well, sir, you stand corrected. I'm with my best mate, drinking vodka and playing snooker with Ronnie and Keith, and I will soon be going out on stage to thousands of screaming fans. It doesn't get much better than that – unless, of course, you throw in a couple of dancing girls and several bags of cheese-and-onion crisps.'

'Fancy a game, boys?' Ronnie asked, handing us two full glasses.

Kelly had mentioned to him that I was quite a useful player in my younger days – another proud badge of a misspent youth in the Cynon Valley.

There were cues already lined up for us. A normal-sized one for me and a small, child-sized one for Kelly. Sorry, only messing. I got ready to break.

Keith wandered over to me, joint dangling on the edge of his lips, and whispered, 'You ate my shepherd's pie, didn't you?' He chalked his cue and turned away.

How weird is that? All I could think of as I was about to hit the white ball was Mick Jagger, the writer of classic hits like 'Brown Sugar' and 'Sympathy for the Devil', rushing from our dressing rooms the night before to inform his long-serving guitarist that I had scoffed some of his precious shepherd's pie! It seemed too unbelievable for words. I guess that, if you have been together for as long as these guys, winding each other up is the kind of excitement they need to get them through the constant pressure and boredom of another world tour.

I broke, but potted the white. I could see 'the Governor' winking at Ronnie. I bet they had been planning to unnerve me all along.

During the third set, Keith's daughters turned up. They were stunning blondes with your typical 'My daddy's a rock star' kind of looks. They were living in Connecticut and were extremely Americanised in their approach to life. They seemed to be intrigued by our accents, especially my deep gravelly Welsh voice, which of course I played on as much as I could.

Keith was very relaxed and we were having a great laugh. He told us he had been born in Cardiff, moved to Cornwall when he was about 6, then moved to London a while after that. Kelly and I had no idea. Keith Richards, Welsh? We, the Welsh nation, should have been screaming this fact from our biggest mountain. We have Tom, Dylan, Burton – and now Richards. What more could you ask for?

'Hey, Dad,' one daughter asked, 'where's Wales?'

Keith stopped in mid-stroke. The lines on his face were more prominent than normal. He placed his cue down, picked up a marker pen and drew a map on the wall of the United Kingdom.

I often wonder what the French rugby union made of that home-drawn map on the wall after the Stones had departed.

He pointed to the top half of his map. 'That's Scotland.' He shook his head. 'You don't wanna go there!' He coughed and laughed at the same time.

'Oh yes, that's where Braveheart grew up,' the other daughter chipped in. 'Don't the men wear skirts there?' Both girls giggled.

'And that' – he pointed with his cue – 'is Wales.' He turned and potted the yellow ball.

Eventually, the girls left, probably none the wiser after their bizarre geography-cum-history lesson by the new supply teacher, Mr K. Richards, who normally specialised in dressing up like a pirate, playing the catchiest guitar riffs in existence and smoking the odd spliff or six.

We got back to playing serious snooker. We were drawing two each: it was time for the decider. Kelly and I were slightly drunk, which is normally a no-no before gigs. Suddenly, a deadly hush descended on the room as one of the roadies brought in two of Keith's most prized instruments. Kelly nudged me; his eyes were alight. To be truthful, I wouldn't really know a good guitar from one you buy in a Freeman's catalogue, but you could just sense these things were special, very special. Apparently, Keith had had them since the early days. The roadie picked one up as though it were a newborn baby.

Then the scene in the room descended into stupidity. Bemused, we watched as the two rock gods turned into little schoolboys, oblivious of anyone around them. It was great to watch.

Ronnie dragged on his fag and asked, 'Can I play one of them tonight on stage?'

A reasonable request, I thought to myself since they were both experienced guitarists. How wrong could I be? Keith straightened up, which wasn't the easiest thing to do after all the vodka and Bob Hope flying about, and muttered, 'No way.'

'Come on – only a couple of songs.'

'No.'

'Why not?'

Keith stared at him. 'Because you are getting on a bit, and you could slip and break the neck of it.'

I glanced at Kelly and mouthed the words, 'Pot calling kettle black, or what?' I was dying to laugh; I really had to bite my lip hard.

The snooker contest was more or less forgotten, as they continued to go at each other hammer and tongs. Then Charlie Watts came in, the legendary Stones' drummer. He rolled his eyes as if he had witnessed it a million times before and winked at me. Charlie had stood by the side of the stage when we were playing the night before. I liked Charlie at lot: he was a real cool gentleman, a proper, proper guy. He was so graceful. He liked me also, I think. He had introduced me to his wife, anyway, which I have been told was a great honour.

While the two guitarists argued, Charlie and I talked about equipment and what he did on his days off, and discussed other drummer stuff. He informed me that he still had the same drum kit as when he started in 1960. That's quite amazing when you consider the amount of equipment he must have been offered over the years, but it just sums up how down-to-earth the guy was. He was always willing to offer me some sound advice.

Kelly and I were eventually allowed to go back to the rest of our gang. On stage that night we played incredibly well and received some great reviews in the morning papers the following day.

## IT'S ONLY SHEPHERD'S PIE (BUT I LIKE IT)

We finished the short tour supporting the Stones that night. It had been quite an experience. During the after show we asked them for a group photo. We stood with Ronnie, Mick and Charlie while waiting for Keith to join us. I could tell they were getting restless. A large black guy with dreadlocks passed by, carrying some of their equipment.

Mick shouted out: 'Hi, mate, stand in here and pretend you're Keith Richards.'

The roadie dropped the speakers and a big smile spread across the guy's face.

Ronnie turned around, 'Mick!'

'What?' he shrugged. 'Well, he does look a lot fuckin' like him!' Jagger winked at me.

I chuckled to myself all day about the way they constantly ribbed each other. I have some great memories of that tour with the Stones. They are still one of the best bands I have ever toured with, great fun and true rock'n'roll superstars.


After the bizarreness of the last few days with the Stones, I really fancied going home for a while to catch up on a bit of sanity, but John had other plans for us. He had arranged a smaller, more intimate gig in the French capital two days later. It was mainly for some of the important individuals in the music business, the movers and shakers, including journalists, radio and TV producers and magazine editors, to show just how far we had come as a band. I didn't mind, really: it gave us another chance to play for our large contingent of French fans, and of course, the usual couple of pissheads who had travelled over from Cwmaman to see us and get plastered.

## DEMONS AND COCKTAILS

So we had a day off in Paris before the gig. The good news, for me, was that Lisa had flown over to see me. Kelly suggested that we go out for a meal. So he, Becka (Kelly's new girlfriend), Lisa and I sat in a lovely Parisian restaurant overlooking the Seine. The setting couldn't have been more romantic as the music floated along on the warm breeze, but my mind was occupied with one major issue. The girls despised each other with a vengeance and, to be truthful, Kelly and I weren't getting on all that well either. It wasn't unusual on these occasions for the two girls to sit opposite each other like two snarling Siamese cats in a competition to see who could lick the last drop of milk from the bowl. Lisa never really had a bad word to say about anyone, but there was something about Kelly's girlfriend she just didn't like. Words such as *demanding* and *manipulating* were often bandied about behind closed doors.

The meal started off fairly civilised, anyway. The food was great, the wine was even better and we talked about the next album and ideas for the direction of the band. Then Kelly dropped one of his bombshells. He said that he thought we should do another tour in Australia, and quite soon.

'Yes, that would be great, I can't wait to go,' Becka piped up. 'I've never been to Australia.'

'I thought you would be behind it,' I snapped at her.

In my opinion it was quite obvious to me that, since Becka had arrived on the scene, much of our touring seemed to revolve around places she wanted to go. I was quite convinced at the time that if Becka fancied a weekend break at the Minehead fucking Butlin's holiday camp, Kelly would insist we play there in front of the Beaver Club. I had become sick and tired of it and I just wanted a rest, to have some time for myself.

## IT'S ONLY SHEPHERD'S PIE (BUT I LIKE IT)

Of course, Kelly jumped to Becka's defence and told me in no uncertain terms to behave. In turn, Lisa leapt in with all guns blazing and let both of them have it. Becka got so mad she threw a glass at Lisa, hitting her on the shoulder. The restaurant went silent. The four of us got to our feet, squaring up to each other. Wine was tipped and a plate smashed on the floor. We shouted some more abuse at each other before storming off in separate directions.

Lisa and I walked around for a while through the city streets before we went back to the hotel. She was still upset and I was fucking tamping. I decided I needed a drink. Lisa went to bed and I found a bar and sat all night sampling the local brew. Arriving back sometime in the morning, I passed Kelly in the corridor. He muttered something under his breath at me and walked off.

For most of the day, Lisa and I kept ourselves to ourselves. We stayed in the room, went out for something to eat and did some shopping. At 5pm sharp, a brace of taxis turned up at the hotel to take us to the gig. We mingled with the others, ensuring we were nowhere near Kelly and Becka. But, as if by some strange quirk of fate, we got lumbered in the same taxi together. Lisa glared at me as if it were my fault.

To say the atmosphere in the cab was frosty was an understatement. I was sure the driver put on gloves and a scarf to protect himself from the chill emanating from the back seat. I thought he was going to have to stop to de-ice the windscreen – on the inside. The silence was getting embarrassing. Everyone was staring out of the windows.

'Well, at least it's not far,' I whispered to Lisa. 'Only about fifteen minutes away.' She squeezed my arm tenderly.

Then, as if my comments had awoken some god in charge of awkward situations who felt the need to prolong our agony, we hit a traffic jam that held us up for about an hour and a half.

I felt like getting out of the cab and walking to the show, but it was belting down with rain. As you know, I'm not what you might call your typical strong and silent type. Normally, if I go longer than five minutes without actually saying something, either someone in a white coat is checking my pulse to make sure I'm not dead, or some landlord is throwing me out of the pub because I'm completely bladdered. But I couldn't stick it any more. I was in my own private purgatory; I just wanted to yell out, 'Come on, everyone, let's forget about last night.' But I knew by the way Lisa's grip on my arm had gone from a gentle squeeze to a rather painful pinch that I'd better not say anything if I knew what was good for me.

So the entire journey was taken in silence. I can only guess what the driver must have been thinking as he glanced every now and again at us in his rear-view mirror.

We got to the venue and Lisa had arranged to meet some friends and left me. Backstage, the dressing room was full of our mates, members of the crew and quite a few individuals John had invited to see the show. Due to my forced silence in the taxi, I needed to talk and I didn't care with whom, or about what. After a short while, I was back to my normal self again, laughing and joking, and sinking a few beers to calm my nerves.

I had my back to Kelly, talking to Simon the guitar technician. I knew Kelly was listening and, just for the devilry, I made some sarcastic comment about touring and glass-throwing. Kelly went ballistic. He started to scream and shout at me, waving his finger.

## IT'S ONLY SHEPHERD'S PIE (BUT I LIKE IT)

The room went quiet. Everyone was afraid to move. I stood there, open-mouthed. He ranted and raged, his face red with anger. I started to wilt under the unwanted attention; I wanted the floor to open up in front of me and swallow me up. Then something snapped inside me. I thought to myself, 'Hang on a minute, I'm not taking this from him, especially when it started because of his bloody girlfriend and her desire to circle the bloody globe.'

I walked up to him, and gave him the typical South Wales Valleys response that is often used when someone finds themselves with their back against the wall. 'Right, me and you, outside.' I pointed at him. Before he could reply, I grabbed him by the collar and dragged him out into a small courtyard, where crates of beer and other stuff were stored. The door closed behind us.

I turned around in one movement and picked him up by the throat, his legs dangling above the floor. I stared into his eyes. 'Don't you ever fucking talk to me like that again, especially when there's a room full of fucking people we don't know! I don't care who you are.' It was my turn to completely lose the plot.

Unfortunately, like most bands, we have had our bust-ups, our fair share of disagreements. When we weren't the best of friends we were fighting like cat and dog – at least Kelly and I were. Neither of us would have even thought about fighting with Richard; he would have bloody killed the both of us with both hands tied behind his back. But whatever the row, whatever the shouting match, we always did it behind closed doors, out of sight of other people. So Kelly's outburst had really got to me.

I finally loosened my grip on him. Verbally, he came straight back at me. He questioned my commitment to the band and he told me that it seemed to him, and others, that I was more interested in pursuing some of my non-band activities. It was wrong and unfair. I felt like smashing his face in, but, luckily for him, the angel of commonsense suddenly appeared on my left shoulder and whispered, 'You can't; he's the singer of the band and he can't go out on stage with a black eye, or the press would have a field day.'

Even though a little red demon was bouncing about on the other shoulder taunting, 'Never mind all that commonsense bollocks, smack his fucking head in and knock his teeth out', we just continued to stare at each other, chests pumping and blood boiling, until John burst through the door and ended the madness.

We went back into the dressing room to get ready. Most of the crowd who were there earlier had left to take their seats. Apparently, while we were outside ready to take each other's head off, someone had asked Richard if he was concerned with what might happen if one of us got hurt.

'Hurt?' he replied, in his usual no-nonsense approach. 'Neither of them could hit their way out of a wet paper bag.'

We went on stage, still not talking. The crazy thing was that the gig that night was one of the best we had ever played together. Maybe it was the release of the pent-up aggression pumping around our bodies and into our instruments. Maybe it was one of those nights when everything just clicked.

On the short flight back to Wales, John commented to me, 'Perhaps you and Kelly should have a scrap before every concert.' He rubbed his chin, deep in thought like a white Don King.

Although Kelly and I kind of kissed and made up, I soon realised that that night underneath the stars over Paris was the start of the beginning of the end for me and the group, even though I had given my heart and soul to it for all those years. It was more than just disagreements due to the tension of touring: this was getting more serious, more personal.

'Stuart is a larger-than-life, booming, smiling, swearing, hairy lovely man. Everyone who meets him, loves him. He certainly makes an impression. I am still convinced he is Tom Jones's lovechild … Where was Mabel Cable in August 1969? When I think of Stuart, I hear a roaring laugh, "Pagey girl", a fart perhaps and of course "fuckin'nella". It has been an absolute pleasure working with him over the years.'

**Scarlet Page, rock photographer and daughter of Jimmy**

# CHAPTER 9

# STARING AT THE BIG BOYS

The insanity didn't stop with fights between Kelly and me, or with the famous Rolling Stones. I also had the pleasure of spending some off-the-wall times with many other top superstars such as Manchester's favourite sons, or brothers, Oasis. I'm not going to make out for one minute that I was great mates with the Gallagher brothers, but I had my moments with them along the way.

The first time I actually met Liam, the extremely hilarious younger of the siblings, we were staying in a hotel by Holland Park in west London. We were still riding high on our success and we were down in the basement, having a few drinks to celebrate. I went upstairs to get something, and there at the reception desk was the unmistakable Liam, booking in and looking like a true million-dollar rock star. It was already quite late. I didn't find out until later, but apparently, he had been thrown out, again, by his wife, Patsy, and was looking for a bed for the night.

## DEMONS AND COCKTAILS

I rushed down to tell Kelly who I'd seen up in reception, when we heard him stomping down the stairs. His swagger entered the room long before he did. He saw us and to our complete surprise, he suddenly burst into his own version of our hit, 'The Bartender and the Thief'. It was quite bizarre to see the new King of Snarling Rock'n'Roll up on a table, giving his all to one of our songs. It had to be one of the biggest compliments we had ever received in our careers. We stayed locked in the bar like Guinness-swilling vampires until the sun came up and then we all trooped off to bed.

Later that year we were invited to attend the Q Awards. John, our manager, had a phone call from Oasis' manager, Marcus Russell. He wanted to know if we would like a table next to Oasis at the event. I assume that must have been one of the quickest and easiest decisions John has ever had to make.

That night was awesome: Oasis to our left and Keith Richards, Ronnie Wood and their partners to our right. I sat there smug as hell. 'What the fuck am I doing here?' I asked myself. I was surrounded by legends, mingling with the powers of rock.

Anyone who knew us knew that we prided ourselves on how much we could drink. We put ourselves right up there with the best of them, Premier League drinkers. That was until we saw how much alcohol Keith and Ronnie could put away. I soon realised we were only novices in comparison. We may have been in the Premier League but they were playing a different game altogether, the Brazilians of drinking. They finished everything on their table: vodka, Jack Daniel's and the wine. And I was later told that Ronnie had taken it easy because he was supposed to be off the sauce.

Later in the evening, I ended up sitting and drinking quite heavily with Liam. He surprised me by telling me that he had recently had a dream about me. He didn't tell me what it was about, and I'm not sure if I had the starring role in it, or was just an extra. But it wasn't half weird thinking that Liam Gallagher was dreaming about me. He's got a mind like a box of fireworks when he's awake, so God only knows what goes on in his brain when he's sleeping.

He was in a great mood and was telling me some really funny stories and jokes until Kyle Minogue hit the stage. It was long before her cancer issues. He turned to me and said, 'I fucking hate her.' He spat the words out in his thick Mancuniian accent. He then shouted out as loud as he could, 'Oi, you, show us your fucking udders you big fat cow!'

I nearly pissed myself.

Everyone turned to look at him. I wanted to hide under the table; I didn't know where to look. But he didn't give a toss and he started staring everyone down. 'What? *What*?' He motioned towards the people who stared at him, then he turned back to me. 'This is the Q Awards, man. Proper music, proper rock'n'roll. She's not fucking rock'n'roll!' His rant lasted a while longer, and then he just smiled and muttered, 'Oh, fuck it, let's get another drink in.'

I really liked the no-nonsense attitude of Liam and Noel. Noel seemed to be a bit more reserved, but he also had his moments. I remember playing a 60th-birthday tribute concert for John Lennon. It had been organised by George Martin, the old Beatles producer. There were only about a hundred people, but the majority of them were stars: Johnny Marr, Oasis, Sharleen Spiteri from the band Texas, and a slew of others. Kelly and Noel were doing a number and I was playing drums. We were struggling to get the rhythm right. Noel turned and shouted across to me, a bit tongue-in-cheek, 'Oh, Stuart, play that fucking beat you do on that fucking giraffe song!'

I knew straightaway what song he was talking about: 'I Wouldn't Believe Your Radio'. I could see him smirking. Kelly smiled through clenched teeth. I started playing it.

'Yeah that's it. That's the fucking giraffe song.' He started strumming along and singing in a weird voice.

There's always a bit of a Mexican standoff at these kinds of events as far as who goes on when. Unless your name is Elton John and you can pick where the hell you want to go on the bill, you have to fight for the first or the last slot on the show to build your ego.

Sharleen Spiteri thought she should go on first and was making her point quite strongly around the room. Suddenly Noel stopped playing his guitar. He turned to her and said arrogantly, 'Oh, love, how many times have you played Wembley this year?'

She went quiet.

'How many?' he continued. You could hear a pin drop. 'Come on, how many times?' It was painful to watch.

'None,' she finally muttered.

'We've played there fucking three times, so, no, you ain't going on first, we are.' He turned his back on her and carried on strumming his guitar.

She didn't know what to say. I thought to myself, 'You can't say that.' But, on reflection, I guess he could. His band had sold more records than anyone around at that time; they played to sell-out concerts in the biggest stadiums all over Europe and they didn't care who they upset along the way, so maybe he had earned the right. Sharleen shuffled away, and, not surprisingly, Noel did get to go on first.

We were privileged to witness the infamous rivalry between the two Gallagher brothers as well. They argued constantly and took the piss out of each other and their manager, Markus Russell. Liam used to rib him to fuck about a rugby side in Wales called Ebbw Vale that Markus was pumping money into.

'Tell them about that crappy fucking rugby side you bought,' Liam piped up as we all sat around talking.

Liam was in stitches as he listened to Markus explaining to us how he had hired some Tongan rugby players on low wages to play for the team. He said everything was going okay until they started winning. Apparently, when they were losing, the costs were under control. Then someone talked him into introducing a try bonus scheme, which is a deal where you give players who score a try some extra money. Since he had introduced it, the Tongans hadn't stopped scoring. They had nearly bankrupted him.

One of the best stories I heard about Liam was actually one that Noel had shared with Kelly. Apparently, around the time Oasis were just becoming successful with their massive first album *Definitely Maybe*, Noel had moved down to London, where he met U2's Bono one night at a party. Noel invited him back round to his little flat, not thinking in a million years that Bono would take him up on his offer. But, later that night, not only did the singer pull up in a taxi, but on his arm was Annie Lennox from the Eurythmics. Can you imagine two of the biggest rock stars in the world in your house? Noel said Bono was dancing about the front room singing the Oasis song 'Live Forever' at the top of his voice.

Obviously, Noel, being the songwriter and mastermind behind the band, was over the moon. He made an excuse and went to the kitchen to phone his brother to tell him the news about Bono in his front room, singing their song.

Apparently, there was silence on the end of the phone until Liam grunted, 'I bet he can't sing it as good as me.' And then he slammed the phone down.

Now how fucking cool and confident was that? They are two boys from a rundown housing estate in Manchester, who made it bigger than big could be, and it hasn't changed them one bit. I hope they live for ever and become the next Rolling Stones, still touring, producing great tunes and playing fuck with everyone in twenty years' time.

One of the last times I came across the Gallagher brothers was during a Teenage Cancer Trust concert. I was late as usual. When I eventually arrived, Simon was waiting for me outside the dressing rooms, which we were actually sharing with Oasis.

'Thank God you're here, he's not happy.'

'Who?' I asked, thinking Kelly was having a cob on again because I was late.

'Liam,' he replied. 'He's waiting for you. He's refusing to shake anyone's hand until you turn up.'

He went on to inform me that Liam had swaggered in, full of attitude. Kelly said, 'Alright,' and held out his hand.

Liam looked at him and asked, 'Where's your man?'

Kelly looked baffled.

'Don't fuck with me! Where is he? Where's Stuey? Where's your man?' Kelly told him I was coming. Liam then skulked off into the corner by himself. For whatever reason, when I walked in, he seemed to come alive. Maybe he had been dreaming about me again.

'Here's my man, Stuey. Stuey, come here.' He hugged me and we sat down at the back of the room. Then it got even more bizarre. He turned into my own private marriage counsellor or agony aunt. He had heard that my marriage was on the rocks and since his own marriage had also broken up earlier that year, I assumed he now thought he was an expert on the subject of divorce. The advice he gave me was to the point and hilarious.

'The first year is the hardest. After that it's a piece of cake, a walk in the park. Let's have a beer.' And that was that. That was my famous fifteen minutes of marital advice from the great Liam Gallagher. I bet not many people can boast about that.

Ronnie Wood was also a really funny guy. A few months after supporting the Stones in France, we were playing in Dublin and after the show Ronnie took us back to a place called Lillie's Bordello, which was the 'in' place to go in the Irish capital. Ronnie was again off the sauce on doctor's orders. His wife took the responsibility for ordering the drinks during the evening. It was tonic water for him and a gin and tonic for her.

Ronnie sat there with a face like thunder. After a while a band came on and everyone got up to watch them. I could see his face light up. He winked at me and quickly swapped his drink over for his wife's. I thought, 'How old are you?' and smirked to myself. He did that all night long and she never knew the difference.

After a great night we headed back to his house. The place was pure class: a massive, old country retreat set in several acres of land just outside Dublin. Ronnie's paintings covered the walls. I never realised how talented he was in that field. You always hear about musicians who think they are also great artists or actors, but Ronnie is actually a proper artist and he's not bad at playing guitar, either.

He and his wife left us alone for a while. So, being the nosey bastards that we were, Kelly and Lisa and I wandered about having a peek. We were whispering and giggling like teenagers when suddenly Ronnie reappeared, riding on the back of a big fuck-off Great Dane.

'Lester Piggott, eat your fucking heart out,' he yelled in his cockney voice, while slapping the dog's arse.

I was doubled up, laughing. 'Get off him, you bloody idiot.'

'Don't worry, I always do it.' He climbed off the dog, which raced the hell out of there. 'Come and see this.' He led us to the room where his swimming pool was. The thing was enormous.

'Do you like it?' he asked. Then he moved around and made us all a cocktail from the bar situated at the end of the pool. 'What do you think?' he piped up again.

'It's great,' I joked, 'but what if you're at *that* end?' I asked, pointing to the far end of the pool.

He smiled wickedly. 'Come with me.' We followed him, glasses in hands, to the other end. Lo and behold, there was another bar at that end. 'I had one put in at this end as well.' He made us another large drink, while spinning the bottles like Tom Cruise in *Cocktail*.

His missus popped her head in. 'Ronnie, stop showing off and leave them alone.'

'Don't worry, the kids are enjoying themselves,' he cried back.

And he was spot on. What in the world was better than being served cocktails in a large heated swimming pool by the legendary Ronnie Wood?

Another band whom I had the great pleasure of getting to know were the brilliant U2. We had met them when they came to watch us headline Slane Castle in Dublin. After that, we were lucky enough to be asked to support them in 2000. It was the European part of the tour, which started in Copenhagen. When we got there, Bono met us as we got out of the car. He thanked us for coming to join them on the tour, and he said how much of an honour and privilege it was for him, because he really liked the band and our style of songwriting.

I was taken aback by how very humble and nice Bono was. I couldn't believe he had gone out of his way to be there to meet us. But that was only the start. A bottle of Dom Perignon champagne and a few cans of Guinness were waiting for us when we got to our dressing room with a note written by their drummer, Larry Mullen Jr. It explained in detail how to make the perfect black velvet by pouring the Guinness in first and then adding the right amount of champagne. They sent it to our room every night. How classy is that? I have supported some so-called 'big' superstar bands who wouldn't go out of their way to say hello, and here was the biggest band on the planet, meeting and greeting us in their own unique way.

On the first night of the whole tour, we went down to have a look at the arena. I couldn't believe it. There was a priest on the stage blessing it. Apparently, they did the same thing at the start of every tour. I can't imagine what the lucky priest must have told his congregation during Sunday's mass the week before the event: 'Oh, and by the way, everyone, sorry but I won't be around on Thursday: I'm doing something with some pop band called YouTwo.'

I wondered if they had also left a bottle or two of bubbly and some Guinness in the priest's dressing room.

It was kind of bizarre when Bono asked the priest if he would bless us as well. I'm not sure if he thought we needed cleansing. We all stood there, heads bowed, having the man of the cloth dab us with holy water. I probably needed more than a drop of the clear liquid to rinse out all of my sins, but what the hell! It was good for a starter.

That same day, we had a lecture from their tour manager, who was called Rocko. A tough old cookie, but very professional, he sat us down and told us in no uncertain terms that he could make our life easy, or he could be a right bastard. The rules were simple: if we were a minute late for the sound check or the show itself, he would cut out one song from our set.

We all nodded in agreement, but didn't pay much attention to his threat until the second day's sound check, when we *were* a little late.

'That's one song less tonight,' he snapped. We thought he was joking, but he wasn't. We were never late again. In fact, we ensured that we were there for the rest of the checks with time to spare.

It was absolutely boiling in the arena on the first night, stupidly hot. But we did a good show and we were well pleased with the reception we got.

When we came off I remember seeing the girl from the pop group Aqua, the one who sang, 'Barbie Girl'. She was really sexy. Drop-dead gorgeous like you would not believe. She was standing with a bald guy. I think Richard was quite smitten with her and followed her round like a dog with two dicks.

The next stop was Barcelona. I remember having words with U2's security staff after losing my temper when a bouncer locked us in our dressing room while U2 were making their way towards the stage. I had tried to get out to phone my wife, but couldn't, so I banged and kicked the door until a security guard opened it.

'What the fucking hell are you doing?' I yelled at him.

'We're been told to lock all doors when the band are coming this way.'

I was gobsmacked. What if there had been a fire? We would have all been killed. What the hell did they need to lock the door for? What did they think I was going to do? Kidnap Bono, or pinch The Edge's hat and run off with it? Better still, try to break Larry Mullen's leg on the off chance they would ask me to substitute for him. I was ranting at the guy and then the man in charge of security bounded over and stared at me. 'I'll get the band on stage and then I'll come back.' He looked menacing.

I thought, 'What the hell am I going to do now?' I went back inside and sat near Richard just in case it got nasty. Five minutes later, the bloke called me out and apologised. He shook my hand and said, 'Hey, man, I like your attitude. If you ever stop being a drummer, give me a shout and I'll give you a job.'

Months later I met him again on the Rolling Stones tour. I felt great when he yelled out in front of everyone, 'Hey, Stuart, my crazy Welsh guy!'

## DEMONS AND COCKTAILS

In total we did 10 dates with U2 on that leg of the tour. I remember that Bono's old man was seriously ill and he was flying home every night to see him.

We joined back up with U2 in America. It was two weeks after September 11 2001, the attack on the Twin Towers and the Pentagon. It was a strange time. One of the first shows was in Madison Square Garden in New York. When we got there, this time every member of the band thanked us for coming; they knew how hard it was to travel around at that time. My wife didn't want me to go, my son Cian was only little, and to be honest, part of me didn't want to go, either. It was hard getting on a plane to the States after it had happened; the world had gone mad and people no longer trusted each other. In the end, I'm glad I went. It was an experience I wouldn't have missed for the world.

That night I watched U2 performing on stage. It was incredible. Not only was I impressed with their show, but also the number of stars who were there to see them: David Bowie, Michael J. Fox, Kathleen Turner, to name just a few. I think it was easier to say who *wasn't* there. U2 are such a huge band. Anybody who was anybody had turned out to see them. They also pulled off one of their masterstrokes, the sort that only they could get away with: they got half of the fire brigade and half of the NYC police force up on stage for the last song. It was the Irish connection.

They played 'One' and all the names of the people who had died on that tragic day were displayed in a roll of honour on the massive backdrop. I was standing there reading them and I felt tears welling up in my eyes. It was so emotional. Fucking hell, it was so hard to take in. The planes had flown into the towers only

**174**

TURIN, ITALY
BOILERSUITASTIC

*Top*: The 'Pick a Part' video shoot in Turin, Italy.

*Above right*: Getting a platinum disc for our second album, 'Performance and Cocktails'.

*Below*: Kelly and me sharing a story and a few beers.

© *Julian Castaldi*

We certainly knew how to relax! Playing pool and watching the rugby with
Kelly and Richard.

*Above*: Travelling on the overnight train from Glasgow to London during filming of the 'Just Looking' video.

*Below*: Me and Melinda Messenger.

© *Julian Castaldi*

*Left*: Me and Nicola… young and in love.

*Below*: Where's my old headmaster to see me flying around in a Lear Jet? How rock and roll is that? © *Julian Castaldi*

*Above*: Trying to be the Welsh Angus Young.

*Below*: On the set of the video shoot of 'Mama Told Me Not To Come' with the one and only Tom Jones.                    © *Julian Castaldi*

*Above*: Supporting U2 in Barcelona.

*Below*: This radio stuff is hard work!

© *Tanya Jones*

*Top*: Drumming with the new band, Killing for Company.

*Above right*: Out on the town with Howard Marks and Rob Brydon after my TV show.

*Left*: Partying with the main man in Cardiff, 2008.

© *Julian Castaldi*

*Above*: Cian – my pride and joy.

*Below left*: Me doing my bit for Oxfam against gun crime.    © *Julian Castaldi*

two weeks earlier; it was still smouldering at Ground Zero when we went to look at it the next day. I'm sure the arena must have been full of people who had family and friends killed in the assault. U2 really know how to pull on the heartstrings. Pope Bono and the rest of the archangels are very good at things like that. Being from Ireland, I think that they could relate to all the terrorism madness. The closest I have ever come to terrorism was Billy Dunn's arch being ripped down from the football field, so I couldn't really empathise like them.

After the second show at the Garden, we were invited to the 40th-birthday bash for their American booking agent. They used to invite us everywhere and, no matter what was going on, our names were always on the guest list. The booking agent's name was David Moose, and again, like most of the backroom staff surrounding the group, he had stayed loyal to them from day one and vice versa. That's another thing I admire about U2. They have surrounded themselves with the same people from the very start. They are all 'One' big family.

The party was planned to take place in a hip venue called Man Ray's. Bono had personally come to see us to ask us if we would like to come. 'No, sorry, Mr Bono, I'm staying in tonight to curl my hair,' I thought of saying, but quickly decided otherwise.

Of course we went. Wild pit ponies couldn't have stopped us. We walked down the steps into the club. On the left was the restaurant area, to the right was the bar. U2 were on the top table. There was one table left at the back, so we piled in. It was a U-shaped booth type of thing. Kelly went to the toilet, Tony and Richard went outside for a smoke and John was by the bar getting the drinks in. I was sitting there on my Jack Jones, texting on my phone, when this strange-looking guy came over. 'Excuse me, excuse me, is anyone sitting here?' he asked in a very feminine voice.

'Yeah, and they'll be back now.' My reply was to the point.

'So, no one can sit down here?' he asked again.

I looked up at him. 'Look, butt, I told you the seats are taken. Don't you understand?'

He shrugged and muttered: 'Well, I'll have to tell Demi Moore there's no room.'

I stopped playing with my phone. 'Excuse me, who did you say?'

'Demi Moore.'

'Oh, if Demi wants a seat, she can sit here, my mates won't mind.'

When I looked up, she was standing there, *the* Demi Moore. She was stunning, her hair short and tight to her head.

She smiled at me and sat down, then said, 'Hey, you're the guy from the support band.'

I nodded my head till it seemed as if it would come off at the hinges.

'By the way,' she continued, 'this is my friend.' From out of the shadows popped Sandra fucking Bullock, and she sat down on the other side of me. I was gobsmacked, my mouth open wide. I was thinking, 'Hang on a minute … I bet I'm being fucking set up here.' I pictured a camera crew filming me from the kitchen.

But I didn't really give a toss if they did show me on one of those fly-on-the-wall, piss-take programmes and everyone in the world laughed at me. I felt as if I'd died and gone to heaven! I had Demi Moore on one side, Sandra Bullock on the other. Never mind seeing me play snooker with the Rolling Stones, where was my old headmaster when I really wanted him?

I spied Kelly coming back. I knew he loved Demi Moore, so I excused myself and rushed to meet him. I couldn't get the words out fast enough: 'Kelly, you won't fucking believe who's sitting on our table?'

I could see him rolling his eyes. 'Who?'

'Only Demi Moore and Sandra fucking Bullock.'

I'm not sure why I kept adding the word 'fucking' in between Sandra's first and last names. Maybe it was a Freudian slip.

I think he thought I was pissed or stoned until he looked across and saw them. The rest of the guys came back and we all sat together getting drunk. Both ladies were a good craic. I recall Demi messing with John Brand and telling him to pout his lips while she pretended to put lipstick on him with what I thought was a tube of the stuff. She was messing about, smearing it all over his lips, and then she popped it in his mouth. It was only when she pulled it out that we all realised it was not her lipstick at all. It was a mini vibrator.

You should have seen the look on John's face. You should have seen the look on all of our faces. John had Demi Moore's pocket rocket in his gob. I don't think he washed his face, or brushed his teeth, for a month after that.

Just as it was getting interesting, my big mouth messed things up yet again. I went to the bar and bumped into Bono.

'Fair play to you, fellow,' I said. 'You throw a great party.' And I went on to boast to him who we had sitting with us.

'Where is she?' he seemed excited. And, sadly for us, that was it. He swooned over with me to our table, and within two minutes, our Demi and our Sandra were whisked off by the Godfather to the table at the top of the room.

What a shame. I'm sure she had the hots for me, too!

Prior to our touring with U2, Keith Duffy from Boyzone informed me that the U2 singer was great when it came to matchmaking. When I asked him what he meant, he simply smiled and said, 'Just try it. If you fancy someone, tell Bono and you will be amazed at the results.'

So one night we were in Philly and I saw this girl in the after-show party. I mentioned to Bono that I thought she was lovely, but I was too shy to talk to her. He smiled at me and told me to follow him. We walked towards the girl. He whispered something in her ear and then put our hands together. 'You two were made for each other. I can feel it; I can see it in your eyes.' It was all nonsense, but it worked a treat. What was a girl to do? She was powerless to resist. He winked at me and walked – sorry, floated – away, leaving me and the girl chatting.

I bet he could walk on water if he wanted to.

After the show in Philly they offered to fly us back to New York in their private plane because the weather was really bad. In a show of Cwmaman solidarity we declined because we thought it would be unfair for the rest of our crew to travel all through the night in our old shitty tour bus while we flew with the Irish megastars. John was fuming because we refused the offer. Looking back, I think it was a big mistake. It wouldn't have harmed for one trip, and the bus journey was a nightmare from hell. Our bus broke down and got flooded near the Brooklyn Bridge.

They didn't hold it against us, though. In fact, I think they liked us because of the fact that The Edge was Welsh (his aunt and uncle were from Llanelli). I remember all of us drinking in Copenhagen and they told us about the night they had played at Cardiff Arms Park in the eighties and they decided to have The Edge kick a rugby ball into the crowd to show everyone his Welsh roots.

'It sounded a good idea at the time,' Bono laughed, 'until The Edge in his cowboy boots kicked it straight into the lighting rig and nearly killed one of the technicians on the spotlight.'

On another occasion Kelly was being really naughty and a little nosy. He actually steamed open a letter that Jools Holland had given him to pass on to Bono. Jools wanted Bono to sing on his new album. He also said in the letter that he believed Bono would enjoy the Stereophonics because they were three great guys and told him that he should get Stuart the drummer talking, because he had the most captivating and interesting speaking voice he had ever heard. Kelly was pissed off with it, but it was his fault for opening it in the first place.

The last story I really remember about touring with U2 happened during one of the first New York shows. Huey from the Fun Lovin' Criminals turned up to be with us. We were good friends with him and his band. He was the one who used to take us to the mad club, and about whom the song 'Roll Up and Shine' from *Performance and Cocktails* was written. Trust it to be his local drinking hole! The place was mental.

We had two dressing rooms, one main room and a shower room we used to call the smoking room, where we would have an occasional puff of blow from time to time. Drugs weren't the thing when gigging with U2. When Huey turned up, he asked if he could smoke some of his weed. He always smoked it neat with no tobacco and his spliffs stank the place out. It nearly got us into trouble in more ways than one. We were in the dressing room, puffing away, and Huey was just about to pass the joint to me when in walked the Mayor of New York. Huey stood to attention, and threw the joint into sink. I didn't know the guy from Adam and I calmly said, 'Alright, mate.' Everyone thought I was a complete lunatic. I was sitting with a towel around me. Apparently, Huey still tells the story about my just sitting there nonplussed, talking to the Mayor as if he were the janitor.

Apparently, outside in the corridors Paul McGuinness was marching through, screaming: 'Who the fuck is smoking Bob Hope?' He bumped into John. 'John, I hope it's not your boys.'

'No, they never touch the stuff,' he commented, then scurried off to see what the hell I was up to.

But that was probably the worst of my memories on tour with U2. We had a great time. They were a real class act and fully deserve to be regarded as one of the best rock bands ever.

---

### SPENDING ON THE ROAD OF ROLL'N'ROCK EXCESS

As I said, early on I was taught to grow up to respect the value of money, but now and again, I would see something I really wanted and treat myself. The main things I bought other than a few houses dotted around the place were the following:

A HARLEY-DAVIDSON: It is my pride and joy. Harleys are

the coolest bikes on the planet. And you can't be a 'proper' rock star if you haven't got one. I once hired one and rode it from

LA (where the band and I were staying in the music producer Trevor Horn's place in the hills, recording tracks for our album) to Las Vegas to watch Tom Jones perform. I saw him in a hotel for one night, had a few beers, put 20 pence in the slot machines and drove back. Absolute paradise.

A RANGE ROVER VOGUE: It cost me 55 big ones – a lot for a car – but it was so beautiful I would have married it. But, as with all of my cars, after a while I got bored and let it go.

A RUGBY SHIRT: I've always loved rugby and one night I went to a charity auction in the CIA (Cardiff International Arena). I had my eye on a Welsh rugby shirt signed by the entire Glam Slam team of 1976. These guys were the most famous team in Welsh history – Gareth Edwards, Phil Bennett, all my heroes. I was over the moon when I won it, until I woke up the next day and saw how much it had cost me. My advice to anyone going to an auction is never, *ever* get drunk and don't try to show off! Seventeen thousand pounds is an awful lot of dosh.

BONNIE SCOTT'S AUTOGRAPH: I paid 2 grand for the

signature of my all-time hero from a collector in Swansea. It took him a year to track it down for me, but it was worth the wait. I also recently acquired the great man's death certificate from a friend of a friend.

# CHAPTER 10

# MY ARSE AND I

Things started to deteriorate between the band and me not long after the fight in Paris. It all came to a head when I refused to go to Japan with them to do a few shows. I was pissed off at the thought of travelling all that way and staying for two weeks just to play two shows – especially when I wasn't feeling well and I honestly thought it was just another trip orchestrated so Becka could go to another destination she had never seen.

That's when the rot really started to kick in and the bad blood between us began to flow. It got to the point where I couldn't even stand to have a conversation with Kelly any more. But it wasn't so bad with me and Richard. To be truthful, he never said too much to anyone, anyway.

They had both travelled to Canada from Japan to play some acoustic gigs, for which I wasn't required. I later found out that Kelly had joked with the crowd that they were missing their drummer because he was in rehab for cocaine abuse.

## DEMONS AND COCKTAILS

My plan was to fly out to San Francisco to meet back up with them for a series of gigs on the West Coast and New York. I was flying upper class with Virgin and was sitting at the onboard bar making conversation with an elderly couple who were originally from Porthcawl in South Wales. We were having a drink together while catching up on life when a terrible pain started throbbing at the bottom of my spine and I couldn't stop scratching it; it was driving me crazy. The woman couldn't help but notice my discomfort and asked, 'Are you okay? You seem to be in some pain.'

I was a little embarrassed to tell her what was wrong, so I just laughed it off and told her it was nothing. A few drinks later, the pain became worse and was moving down towards my back passage. I confessed to them that I thought there was something wrong with my arse, which is never an easy thing to tell anyone, especially a pair of relative strangers on a plane.

'Do you want a suppository?' she offered.

'I wouldn't even know how to use it,' I said, showing my dullness.

She was probably thinking, 'You stick it up your hole, you dull fucker,' but she was much too polite and just explained how it worked.

In normal circumstances I would have thought it a little too strange for a woman to be sitting by a bar in an aeroplane, offering younger men strange things to poke up their rectums, but I was in really bad pain and desperate, so I went to the toilet and fiddled with it until it disappeared where the sun didn't shine. It felt really peculiar to say the least and the experience of shoving the cold, hard plastic tube up my behind was all for nothing, because it didn't help at all.

## MY ARSE AND I

For the rest of the flight I tried to cope with the increasing pain by continuing to occupy my seat by the bar and drinking as much alcohol as I could without passing out.

When we landed I got a cab. It was as humid as hell on a cool day and I couldn't sit down on my arse properly. I'm sure I was a sight to behold. When I got to the hotel I was a bit the worse for wear and went straight to bed. Hours later, I woke up in agony. I was really worried then. My ring piece was throbbing as if I'd eaten the hottest vindaloo in history.

The boys arrived from Canada a few hours later. They came to see me and I told them about my problem. The way I was feeling, drumming was the last thing on my mind.

'We'll have to get Steve Gorman [from the Black Crowes] in,' said John.

'Why?' I asked. 'What does *he* know about arses?' I thought. I must have been delusional due to the pain because I actually thought for one eccentric minute he was suggesting they get Steve Gorman so he could inspect my rectum.

I could hear the imaginary conversation playing out in my head: '"Fucking hell, man, that looks painful," the drummer said to me as I bent over.'

'Never mind that, do you know what it is?' Kelly asked. 'We have a show to do tonight.'

'It looks like he's eaten a fucking alien.'

It was too painful to laugh at that thought, and I was too restless to cry.

Back in the real world, John explained that he actually meant they would have to get Steve to do the show, not look at my arse. I was relieved. I had images of them dragging in a host of other drummers such as Ringo Starr, Cosy Powell and Animal from *The Muppets*, until one of them could diagnose the condition.

I stayed in bed while they did the show that night. Next day we had a long bus trip to LA. Normally I loved going to the Golden State because it's so laidback, but I wasn't in the mood this time. To be truthful, I just wanted to go home and curl up in bed. I could hardly walk by then. A doctor turned up, and after giving me a brief examination, prescribed some strong painkillers. I necked them down as if I was eating Smarties.

Two days of agony later, I was getting really concerned. I could barely walk at all. I had to crawl across the room to go to the bathroom and I could feel something dangling down from my hole like my very own hanging baskets of Babylon.

I showed John Brand.

'Bloody hell! Have you seen it?' he muttered, rather shocked.

'No, I can't see it.' I answered him back sarcastically.

He told me there appeared to be a big, swollen bag of pus protruding from my rectum. John got me in to see a guy in Beverly Hills. The taxi ride was horrendous; every hump and bump in the road sent pains shooting from my hole up to my brain. It's funny looking back now, but every time I think about Beverly Hills I don't automatically picture lovely big houses with massive swimming pools: I picture myself clambering out of the cab and inching my way like a giant crab up the steps to the doctor's office. I thought I was going to faint.

The doctor was called Hoffman and he was tremendous. He helped me up on the table and had a good, long look. 'Oh, yeah, I can see what it is and don't worry, Stuart,' he told me. 'I've been looking at asses for 15 years and my old man's been into them for

35.' It was his 'arse doctor' (or 'ass doctor') sense of humour. I was dying to laugh, but it hurt way too bad.

He brought his father in just to check on his diagnosis. They both concluded I had something called a perianal abscess, which is a collection of pus outside the anus. It arises from an infection in the lining of the anal passage, which leads to inflammation and abscess formation.

I didn't know if it was their analysis or the fact that two strangers were poking and prodding me in my forbidden planet that upset me more.

'What are you going to do with it, Doc?' I grunted. 'Can you lance the bugger?'

He looked at me as if I had two heads, or in language he understood, two arseholes.

'Lance it? If I pricked that, my boy, the pain would be so excruciating you would hit the ceiling. Not to mention it would be extremely messy.'

'Oh.' I didn't like the sound of that. 'Shall I come back in a few days?'

He shook his head. 'No, we need to operate now, straightaway.'

Operate? I was scared. I was about to go under the knife, a million miles from home and alone. Meanwhile, the boys and John were preparing for the gig.

About ten minutes later, a crazy-looking guy with a long ponytail entered. 'Hey, man, I've been told you're a rock drummer.' He looked like a throwback to the early '70s. He gave me a high five. 'I'm here to give you your premed, man.' I thought he was a lunatic who had just come in off the street but he turned out to be the anaesthetist.

'Only in America,' I thought, but 'Only in LA' was more like it.

He pulled two syringes from behind his back. 'Okay, man, which one do you want, the general or the local anaesthesia?'

'Which one's the best?' I replied.

'If I was you I would go with the general. It will knock you right out.' He smiled before pumping it into my arm. It didn't take long to start to take effect.

He wheeled me down to the operating theatre. When we got there I could hear music playing: it was Led Zeppelin.

'Thought I'd put some rock on for you, man.' The guy danced around the room playing air guitar.

I tried to imagine something like this happening on the National Health Service, but then I finally blacked out, and woke up some time later. The doctor came in to see me. He told me to try to walk about. I gingerly got out of bed and walked a few paces. I still felt a bit tender down below but it didn't hurt like before. I shook his hand and thanked him. It was the most pain-free stroll I had taken in about eight days.

He sat me down and explained what he had done. He drew my anus on a piece of paper and explained in detail about the perforated lining and how he had cut the abscess out and fixed any other damage. He told me it was a common occurrence in drummers because of all the movement and the sweating. 'But don't worry, I had a good rummage about up there and everything else seems fine.'

'So in layman's terms, Doc, you've been sticking your finger in me,' I inquired.

He corrected me: 'Fingers, Mr Cable, fingers.'

## MY ARSE AND I

I came back a day or so later to have the dressing removed. It was almost as painful as the abscess. I noticed several gold discs in his office that had been given to him by many a good rock star who had come to see him over the years to get their private bits sorted by the great Dr Hoffman from Beverly Hills. He was a top bloke, and before I left, I thanked him from the bottom of my arse.

I met back up with the band. To be fair, they were really concerned for me. We had only one show in Chicago, then two nights in New York left to play, so they suggested it would be better if I went straight home and got myself ready for the European part of the tour, which was kicking off in two weeks. I didn't argue. All the mental and physical stress had taken its toll on me. I made a promise with myself to get fighting fit and ready to play again as soon as possible.

When I arrived home from LA after having my arse exorcised, I went back to my house in Wales. I still wasn't feeling 100 per cent, and although Nicola didn't have to because of all the things I had done to her, she looked after me and made sure I was okay. It was nice to spend some time back in familiar surroundings and have Cian around to cheer me up.

When I landed, John Brand contacted me with the news that he had been sacked. I knew he and Kelly weren't seeing things eye to eye, but it was still a shock. Maybe it was the start of the revolution.

On the Saturday night, I had a phone call from our new manager, Dan.

'Everything okay, Stu? Trip back alright?' He made some small talk.

**189**

I had a feeling something wasn't right. He oozed insincerity, and I could hear the knives being sharpened.

He added, 'We have a small problem. Due to your medical problem we can't get insurance for you to drum on the European leg of the tour.'

There was silence. I was baffled.

'What do you want me to do?' I demanded to know. 'Should I phone around for a quote?' I pictured myself going on the Internet and Googling 'insurance', and then scrolling down the list of different policies available: car insurance, home insurance, dog and other pet insurance. Oh, here it is: insurance cover for drummers with bad arses – 100 per cent no-claims bonus needed!

I didn't know what he wanted me to do. 'You manage the band, not me,' I snapped at him. 'And by the way, there's nothing wrong with me. I have a letter from the doctor that says it's a common issue with drummers.'

He told me to leave it to him and he would see what he could arrange. But I had a feeling something was up; there was definitely something more sinister behind his bizarre call.

The night after, I was still jetlagged and trying to keep awake when my mobile phone rang again. This time it was Richard. He's not the best of talkers at the best of times. 'Arrggg … oh … alright, butt … arrrgggg … ohhhhh,' he stuttered.

I soon concluded it was either an obscene phone call, or there was something he was having a really hard time telling me. I knew it was the latter.

'Richard, put Kelly on, butt – you're fuckin' rubbish.'

I could hear some mumbling in the background and then there

was silence before Richard came back on, 'He'll phone you back.' The line went dead.

I walked out to my car because the reception was crap in my house. I waited. My heart beat wildly in my chest. The phone rang. It was the little, big man himself. 'Hiya. That's it, butt. It's all over: you're out.'

I knew it was coming, but it was still a bitter pill to swallow. 'Thought so,' I replied.

'What do you mean?' He seemed surprised.

'Look, Kel, I'm not a dull boy.' I was going to mention my GCSE qualification in metalwork, but I thought I'd keep it up my sleeve for later.

He then had the nerve to inform me that it hadn't been an easy decision and that he had been crying for the last few nights because it would mean he would never see my face on the tour bus again.

'Oh, my heart bleeds for you,' I wanted to scream at him. I was the one getting booted out of the band that I helped to start. I thought I would end up signing on the dole and becoming the biggest laughing stock in Cwmaman, and he expected me to feel sorry for him because he'd been crying. 'Fuck you! Go and write me a sad song,' I wanted to spit back at him.

But things like that just summed up Kelly to a T for me. He was always turning things around to him, always trying to be the centre of the universe. The world revolved around Kelly Jones, Chapter One Hundred and Thirty-fucking-Two.

'Stu,' he added, 'it was me and Richard's decision.'

'Okay, that's cool.'

'Aren't you pissed off, then?'

'No. You knew I wanted to leave.' I put a brave face on it. In fact, I had been thinking I would make a break in the next couple of months to branch out and do some other stuff.

The only thing we agreed on that night was that we would all meet up when they got back and sort out a press statement together and release it. In my mind it was all going to be done very civilised, like.

I didn't tell a soul except for John Brand. He was gobsmacked when I phoned him; he had a feeling his time was up with the band, but he didn't think in a million years they would get shot of one of their most important ingredients. He advised me to get a lawyer as soon as possible. So, on the Monday morning, after a few phone calls, I headed to London to speak to my new lawyer, Richard Bray.

It was the Tuesday morning after the phone call. I was due to meet my lawyer when I had Merthyr's finest son, Owen Money, phoning from BBC Radio Wales to ask, was it true that I had been sacked? As I mentioned earlier, I was too shocked to speak to him and put the phone down.

I still couldn't believe they had done this to me. It made my skin crawl and goose pimples were racing up my spine. I will never forgive Kelly or Richard until the day I die. In fact, I told Kelly when I met him much later that I would stamp on his grave for doing what he did to me. I would stamp on it singing Coldplay songs.

I phoned Kelly straightaway. Obviously, he didn't answer his mobile. I expected as much. Next on my list I contacted a woman from the band's press office, Terry Hall. I went mental on her, yelling and screaming. She tried to say she didn't know anything about it, which in my opinion was complete rubbish. I threatened to sue the arse off the band and her for how the situation had been handled. Things got worse when I found out the boys had posted statements on the band's official website. I phoned the record company and threatened to come round to the offices with a baseball bat if they didn't give me my say, or take their biased comments off the website. They removed their comments within twenty minutes.

The gloves were off, and all friendships were off, too. I rushed to meet my lawyer and, in the words of the great Liam Gallagher, 'My lawyer was fucking mad for it.'

'We can take them all the way: six-figure sum, maybe seven,' he explained to me.

For a while after that, Kelly and I had a running text battle. It started about two weeks later when I went to see AC/DC playing at the Hammersmith Palais in London with John Brand. After the gig we were having grub in some restaurant when I received a text from Kelly asking how the gig was. I thought, 'You cheeky, selfish wanker. You just sacked me and now you're pretending everything's normal and we're the best of mates.' I texted back and more or less told him where to go. The next morning he sent me the longest text message I have ever seen. It was the *War and Peace* of text messages, and it must have cost him about £500. It was a full rant, telling me I lacked commitment and how it was my own fault, how I hadn't treated him like a friend for four years and, basically, I was a lazy fucker. It also went on to say that I had also been sacked from all my other jobs and at least I would receive royalties from the band, etc., etc. Then, bizarrely enough, he ended it with, 'I love you and take care'.

The hate texts went back and forth like a tennis ball for a while and then we made no contact until the lawyers stepped in. That's when it all kicked off. It was a full year and a half of total and utter bollocks, guerrilla tactics and germ warfare. When you start out in a band with a glint in your eye and a dream of making it big, the last thing you ever think about is sitting opposite two of your best 'mates' in a roomful of fucking lawyers discussing, and arguing, about money. It was probably the most bizarre thing in my life to be there with my friends, but not to be *with* them. There was the odd nod of the head now and then, but no smiles, no hugging each other, just business — the business of fucking each other over, breaking up our lives, cutting our friendship up into little pieces and scattering them all over the floor.

Kelly, and probably the record company, insisted on keeping the name of the band, even though I had thought of it. I could have contested it, but hell, what was I going to do with the name? Form a tribute-style band and call it Stuart Cable's Stereophonics? Bollocks to that! I'd had enough of playing things like 'Local Boy in the Photograph' and all the crap that went with it, anyway.

The entire legal process took an age to complete and was very expensive for both parties. There were lots of arguments and discussions about whether we were a limited company or a partnership, who owned shares, who held the most and who *should* hold the most, lots of shit like that. It was brain-numbing. I just wanted to scream out, 'Why are we doing this? We are the Stereophonics. Nothing else — *nothing else* —

matters.' But it did matter; the rules of the game had changed, changed for ever.

On advice, I went for a big pay-off. Obviously, they came in with a much lower offer, *much* lower. Then the games and the bartering started. It was like a sketch from Monty Python's film, *The Life of Brian*. 'How much will you give me for this gourd?'

Everyone was trying it on: my lawyer, their lawyers. It became a chess game as we all tried to screw each other. Neither side could agree and it looked as if it was going to go to arbitration until suddenly they came up with an offer that was somewhere near what I was looking for. I agreed to accept. Later on, my lawyer told me that Kelly had wanted to give me more from the start, but Richard had opposed it. I'm not blaming Richard and I don't think it was anything personal against me; it was just that Richard would have been busted and I don't think he really had a pot to piss in, as they say. Kelly was the one making the big bucks. He was the songwriter, and the credits had been changed over the last few albums to show exactly that.

So, when it was all done and dusted, I came out with a handsome sum. Not as much as I wanted, but more than I really thought I would get. Also, of course, I still get the royalties from the records I was involved with and money from performing rights. It wasn't millions, but it kept the wolf from the door.

And yet, to me, it wasn't about the money. For anyone who's ever been lucky enough to play in a band in front of a crowd, be it ten people or fifty thousand bouncing fans singing your songs at the top of their voices, you know it's not about the money. All the money in China can't buy that feeling – or is it all the *tea* in China? Whatever. I'm still not sure why the three of us just couldn't have sat down in a room and sorted it out without the lawyers and all the bollocks that went with it. And the crazy thing was, if I had walked away, which I was strongly considering doing anyway without being pushed, I would have only got about £80,000 at most.

It hadn't been an easy time, going through the legal stuff. I sat on the train on the way home and found myself daydreaming about the beginning: the day a very much younger Kelly knocked on my door to ask me to play with him; the time Richard walked into his first rehearsal, looking all cool and handsome; the night we conquered Cardiff Castle, and all the other great things we had done together. Where had it gone wrong? Why had it all changed?

To be honest, yes, I had had a hand in my own downfall, but I don't believe I lacked 'commitment' to the band. What does commitment actually mean, anyway? How do you measure it? And I definitely wasn't more interested in my TV career than being a rock star. I always did the TV stuff when I had time off, and it was agreed by all of us.

I think Kelly neglected to look in the mirror when he sacked me, most likely citing my lack of commitment for the band's failure to achieve superstar success. Although I think he should be regarded as one of the best songwriters in the country, I really believe his lack of pure frontman coolness, his obsession with achieving superstar status and his intense personality, on and off the job, were just as much to blame.

Kelly had really changed from the early years. When he realised we weren't moving up to the next division it started to alter him. He was obsessed with achieving the recognition that bands such as Oasis and Coldplay were getting at the time. After the second album, it started to become the Kelly Jones Show; it somehow seemed to turn into his band. He wrote the songs, sang them, arranged all the music, told me what drum beats to add, and, as a matter of fact, he also got most of the royalties. Maybe we should have changed our name to Kelly Jones and the Stereophonics.

In my view, I think it was also his rationale behind tinkering with the line-up between the making of the third and fourth albums. We went from a three-piece band to a four-piece, then a five-piece, then back to a three-piece. I think he thought the changes in personnel would make the band suddenly become superstars. He neglected to think that maybe he was the one who needed to change, not the line-up. He was the one doing all the singing, all the writing, he was the front man.

Unfortunately for him, he's not the same type of frontman as Bono. He's not smooth like Noel Gallagher or a showman like Robbie Williams in front of the public. He may have the looks and the talent but he just didn't have that 'something' you need to take it to the next level. During interviews he was uptight and tense, and the reporters knew how to push his buttons. I've been there when they would have a go at him or make a sarcastic comment, and instead of leaving it go he would always bite, always come back aggressively. Often it would turn into a pissing contest with the press and I think it hurt us in the end.

I thought back to the time he was on *Friday Night with Jonathan Ross*, which is a really good example. We were flying in from somewhere in Europe and he wanted me to go on the show with him. I would have loved to have been on the show, but Nicola had just had Cian and I needed to get home to help her.

On the plane beforehand, I recall saying to Kelly that he'd better watch himself during the interview because JR was a quick-witted fucker, who could tie his guests up in knots if he wanted to. Kelly told me that he could handle it. During the interview Jonathan asked Kelly something like what it was like being a Welsh bloke now living in London.

To this day, I still don't know why he blurted out his now notorious reply of, 'I'm as Welsh as a doner kebab.' I was at home watching the show at the time and I couldn't believe he'd said that; I could only begin to imagine what all the Welsh people must have been thinking. Apparently, the regulars in the Ivy Bush were tamping and threatened to rip his photo down from the wall.

This was the country that had given us our first break; it had provided us with more support than any other Welsh band ever. It had also given us our biggest gigs and our biggest pay days, and he came out with something as stupid as that.

Knowing him, I think he probably blamed me for the slip-up, because I had just, weeks beforehand, told him where the saying had originally come from. I had read an interview in a newspaper that featured Griff from the Super Furry Animals. He was asked what he thought of the then very much alive Diana, Princess of Wales. Griff, being a very patriotic Welshman, told the reporter that she was not the princess of our country because she was about as Welsh as a doner kebab. Now, in that ironic context, I can fully understand it, and without sounding like a Welsh extremist, it made perfect sense to me. But what the hell Kelly was thinking of when he tried to distance himself from the country of his birth by comparing himself to a slab of spicy meat, sliced from a spit and garnished with salad, was beyond me at the time, and still confuses me even today. Maybe he thought it was what his new mates, or the media people in London, wanted him to say; maybe he believed it would help sell more records, get us to Number 1.

When I met him after the show he was very sheepish. He told me he hadn't said it like that and that it had been edited that way to make him look bad. Why would someone want to do that? In his mind it was all part of the 'Kelly-Jones-gate' conspiracy.

I was later told that Tom Jones wasn't amused with the way his one-time singing partner had belittled his country. To be fair to Tom, whatever people say about him, he's always been proud to be Welsh: he's got red, white and green blood flowing through his veins.

John recognised that the band needed a better connection with the public if it was going to be really successful as well. We had discussed it on several occasions. In fact, he was always pushing to set me up with a microphone when we played live so I could talk between songs and form a bond with the audience. John knew I had the voice and the personality to win people over and to break down the barriers.

One day I had a brainwave that I thought could really help our reputation. We had recently played *The Late Show with David Letterman*. After a few beers I said to Kelly, 'How much do you want America, Kel?' I could tell by his eyes he wanted it bad. 'I'll give it to you, if you want,' I added.

I could see his expression change. 'What do you mean?'

'Look, let me go on shows like *Letterman* by myself and get interviewed. I'll promote the band, I'll do all of the talking.' My logic was that the Yanks loved all that stuff – just look at Dylan

Thomas and Richard Burton. The Yanks loved their deep gravelly voices.

But, as expected, Kelly didn't agree with any of it. Everything needed to be on his terms. If he wasn't the number one and the one leading it, it was a no-go and so the idea died a quick death.

Little things like that will always let him down.

His obsession with superstardom, especially in America, caused major friction within the band. I'm not saying I wouldn't have minded scoring a couple of Top Ten hits that side of the Pond, either, or to have the royalty cheques that go with it. I've been in the mansions of some of their stars who have had a hit or two and it's obscene the money they make. But I also knew that, to break America, we would have had to tour around consistently; it wasn't going to be handed to us on a silver platter. U2 had done all the hard graft before they made it, show after show, city after city, to become what they were in America.

At the time, I didn't really fancy spending half my life travelling aimlessly around that massive country in a tour bus to play in front of a few hundred people. We had already been there a couple of times and we were, more or less, still playing to the same-sized crowds in the same-sized venues. For whatever reason, it just wasn't happening for us. Branson had tried his best, and we supported some big bands over there, such as U2, but we just didn't click with the American public. There was nothing moving, nothing going on. Even when we recorded 'Maybe Tomorrow', which I honestly believed would be a smash hit across the globe, it didn't fly outside Europe.

It got to the stage when I didn't know what the point was. I thought we should have spent more time concentrating on Europe, where we were one of the top bands, with Number 1 albums, lots of radio play and performing in huge stadiums.

And I wasn't the only casualty of Kelly's overly intense personality. It had pushed out John and others besides us, including Julian, our photographer. Kelly had left his old girlfriend Emma and headed for London after the second album. A while afterwards, Julian started to go out with her. Kelly found out and for some reason he went mental. Again, I couldn't understand why. He had been the one to leave her at the height of our fortune and fame. From where I was standing he wanted the penny and the bun. Kelly stormed up to Julian's house and they had a scuffle, which ended with Kelly throwing a brick through the windscreen of Julian's car.

This caused a hell of a lot of grief with the band because I was mates with Julian. I told Kelly I wasn't going to stop bothering with Julian because they'd had a little tiff. I had always been told: never get involved in domestics. The fight was hushed up to save everyone concerned. Then, when it had almost all died down, Kelly went and spilled the beans about the whole thing to Q magazine. I couldn't believe it as I sat there during the interview, listening to it all come out. When Julian read it, of course, he was bouncing and he phoned Kelly straightaway.

Kelly then had the cheek to deny saying it at all. He actually told Julian it had been blown out of proportion by the press and that he had the wrong end of the stick.

Subsequently Julian parted with the band, which was a real shame because he was, and still is, an excellent photographer. When he left we had to buy all the rights to the photographs he had taken over the years for about twenty grand or something like that.

Not long after the incident Julian showed me a three-page email Kelly had sent him one night. It was a full rant, a bit like the text message he had sent me. The email had no full stops, commas or any punctuation at all. It was difficult to read unless you concentrated really hard. I didn't know where the hell his head was.

I still think Kelly is a super-talented guy but he needs to respect people a bit more. I still believe that, as a songwriter, he is one of the best around, very underrated, but as a person, he's sometimes got as much personality as a doner kebab.

'Stuart presented the *Kerrang!* Awards a few times. We'd get together beforehand and run through the script and we'd invariably end up off on a tangent, talking about some obscure song by some dodgy-haired metal band. One year we were presenting an award to Brian May and Stuart was keen to add a joke about their similar hairstyles. We ran through it a couple of times and it didn't sound quite right, but on the night Stuart wanted to ad-lib it. When he stopped the proceedings and asked Brian what kind of mousse he used, he received the blankest expression ever witnessed by man. Stuart stuck to the script after that.

'The year after, for some inexplicable reason, Juliette Lewis wanted to host the show, so we got her together with Stuart for a run-through in K West. She was wired on two huge coffees; Stuart was politeness itself under a barrage of questions like, "And what's penultimate? That's not an American word."

'On the day Stuart pulled it all together, putting his arm around Juliette like her big brother when she struggled with the one-liners, protecting her from the rampant bands so pissed they could hardly stand. To celebrate we made him dress up as a ringmaster the next year. With his top hat, he looked like Slash in an ill-fitting suit, but he managed to keep it on and made Slayer behave themselves too.'

**Dave Henderson, former head of Emap magazines and the guy Stu worked for when presenting the *Kerrang!* Awards**

# CHAPTER 11

# LOST DAYS AND DARK KNIGHTS

I got sacked from the 'Phonics in September 2003. In December that year, they were due to play a massive home coming concert in the Millennium Stadium in Cardiff. Funnily enough, I had actually been contemplating leaving the band on my own after that gig, but it still didn't make the night any easier for me. The feeling of despair I felt as the event happened will stay with me for a long, long time.

I was in my flat in Cardiff. On the day of the concert I could see everything unfolding from my window: the crowds gathering, the distant noise of the sound check, and the lights from the stage show beaming high into the evening sky.

It really hit me for six. In fact, it hit me like a baseball bat right across my head. I felt incredibly sorry for myself. I wanted to curl up into a big, round ball and hide under my blankets until the coast was clear and the nasty little rock star had ridden back out of town.

## DEMONS AND COCKTAILS

I must admit, that night was the darkest time of my entire life. Deep down I knew I should have been there, getting ready in the dressing room, going through my own routine. Me, a bag full of pent-up energy, messing about, talking all of the time and rushing for a last-minute crap. I should have been the one walking out in front of 80,000 screaming people. It should have been me throwing drum sticks into the audience and then blasting into our opening number.

But it wasn't. There was some other drummer perched on my old stool while I sat in my flat picturing every minute of it in my demented mind. Although I wasn't alone, for Lisa was there and a few others had come round to see me, inside I was the loneliest person in the world. I was a stone's throw away from the stadium where they were playing our songs, songs that flowed through my bloodstream, songs locked in my heart. Until that point in my life, I had never ever considered something as stupid as suicide, but that night I could really understand why people get depressed enough to do it. Fortunately, I didn't, because, knowing Kelly as I do, I think he would have probably taken my suicide and with great pleasure turned it into a classic slow-rock song. I could actually hear him singing it in his gravelly voice at my funeral:

> Mabel Cable's second son,
> Blew his head off with a loaded gun.
> Mabel's left with nothing but a Brit Award
> and a signed autograph of Bonnie Scott.

What a bastard Kelly is; even in death he would torment me.

## LOST DAYS AND DARK KNIGHTS

In my flat I could hear the whine of the music as the night progressed. Every time I closed my eyes, I could picture Kelly and Richard bouncing around the stage. So, being who I am, I did the next best thing I could think of and got off my head on booze and coke. I felt as though I were in a film, a fly-on-the-wall documentary.

To be truthful, I don't remember much about the rest of the night, other than that it was long and painful.

The funniest thing is that someone close to the band recently told me that, on the night of the Millennium Stadium concert, Kelly was so concerned I would turn up and play fuck that he hired an extra 25 security guards just in case. I could picture him walking, sergeant-major-like, in front of a long line of bouncers, showing them a photograph of me and saying, 'He's loud, has big hair, he dresses unfashionably and, if you see him, shoot to kill.'

I still don't know if it's true, but if he did, I don't know what the hell he thought I was going to do – parachute into the stadium dressed in a silver suit and packing a ray gun?

At the time of the whole sacking thing, Lisa was a rock for me. She stopped me from drowning in a vat of my own self-pity. But, like an idiot, I messed things up with her, too. The king of fuck-ups, the fresh prince of getting it wrong struck again, and I paid another heavy price for it.

Our love affair ended just as fast as it had started, when Nicola phoned Lisa to tell her I'd been spending time back with her and Cian while she was away doing TV assignments. It was true, but there wasn't anything underhand. When Lisa went away, I basically just went there to see my boy and stayed over a few nights. That one phone call changed everything between us. Lisa lost the trust in me that had once fuelled the flames of our hot relationship.

She contacted me from her parents' house in London and, along with some other chosen words, told me it was over. I was in Cardiff at the time, recording my TV show, and I was so distraught that I jumped in the car immediately. I needed to see her face to face. I drove like a madman up the M4. I met her and we argued. I tried my best to turn the situation around but the trust was gone. She refused, point-blank, to continue with our relationship and that was the end of it.

I will never forget the feeling as I climbed back into my car and looked at her through the rear-view mirror as I drove away. It was painful. I was upset. As I drove home over the Severn Bridge, I remembered the sad tale behind our song 'Billy Davey's Daughter', where the daughter of Billy Davey commits suicide by jumping from the bridge into the cold water below. I felt so low. My mother's advice from some time before was spinning around and around in my nightmare: 'You will end up a sad and lonely old man, Stuart, a sad and lonely old man.'

I decided it was time for me to take action. So I dealt with my situation in the best way I knew at the time. I went back to my flat in Cardiff and entered a world fuelled by drink, women and drugs. I purposely walked through the door of madness. It's hard to explain, but it was something that I needed to get out of my system. I had lost Lisa forever and, although technically I still wasn't divorced from Nicola, for the first time in ages and ages, I was a single man again and I aimed to enjoy every minute of it. Sometimes you have got to go there to get back, as some clever bastard once called an album.

Not long afterwards, I was asked to host the *Kerrang!* Awards in London. I had some friends up in the city, a married couple who said I could stay over at their place for a few nights. The night before the ceremony, the wife made us a meal in their flat. During drinks, the husband told me he'd invited some friends around and he hoped that I wouldn't mind.

'I don't care,' I replied. 'The more the merrier.'

About thirty minutes later two stunning girls turned up, arm in arm. My mouth hit the floor, my host just smiled. They sat either side of me and we had a great time over dinner. I did most of the talking and they just smirked and giggled. After the coffees the coke came out. We did one line after another. Things were heating up, but I knew I had a busy schedule the following day and I didn't want to mess it up. I was hosting the entire *Kerrang!* event from start to finish in front of about a thousand people, including one of my all-time heroes, Angus Young. I knew I needed to be on top of my game but the demon inside me had come out to play and had tied up the angel from my other shoulder and locked him in a cupboard for the night.

My party brain took over, or maybe it was my party penis.

Next thing, my host and his wife went to bed, leaving me with the two beauties. I went to the toilet to consider my next move. I didn't really need a plan because, when I came back out, they were both starkers. One of them was licking the other out in front of the fire as though she were devouring a lollipop. It was like an X-rated scene out of a porn film, but with me as the lucky bastard who got to enjoy it. I stood there, grinning like a spare prick in a lesbian orgy.

'What the hell am I going to do now?' I asked myself. I was

a Valleys boy and things like this didn't happen to people from my neck of the woods. Thankfully, the decision was taken out of my hands.

One of the girls crawled over to me on all fours and started to unzip my trousers. I smiled as she began munching on my old boy. For some reason I thought of Keith Richards. Again, not in an 'I fancy him' sort of way. I just thought, 'I bet Keith Richards wouldn't turn it down, would he?' And I'm not too modest or too sorry to say, I didn't turn it down, either. It was too good a dish, or dishes, to pass up. I ended up in bed with both of them.

Next day at the *Kerrang!* Awards, I walked around like someone who'd come up trumps on the Lottery. During the ceremony I wanted to stop all the activities and shout out, 'Oi, you lot eating your bangers and mash, never mind who won Best Rock Video, never mind the top band, you should have seen what I did last night. I was like the God of Love.'

A few weeks later, a really weird thing happened. One of the girls involved in the *ménage à trois* wrote a letter to *FHM*, saying she had slept with me and I was the 'King of Fuck'. I remember someone phoning me to tell me to get a copy.

'Only one copy?' I thought, 'Bollocks to that! I'm going to buy a thousand and give them to everyone I know.' It was official and it was in print: Stuart Cable is a superstud. I sauntered around like John Wayne for weeks, winking at girls and smiling; I still think I have the clip from the magazine in my wallet. No, I'm only messing. I actually have it next to my Brit Award on the mantelpiece surrounded by flashing lights and a big inflatable pointing finger.

That night was the 25th anniversary of *Kerrang!* magazine and they were presenting an award to the great Angus Young. I really wanted to present the award to him myself, but for some reason they picked a guy to do the honours who knew as much about AC/DC as my two fucking dogs. So I was a little pissed off and went back to stand in the shadows, when they turned out the lights to show the video clip with his achievements.

Everyone in the room was watching the screen when suddenly I felt someone standing by my side. I looked over and saw Angus. My knees were knocking as I held out my hand. 'Well done, Angus.'

'Thanks, Stuart,' he replied. 'Nice to see you again.'

I nearly fainted when he not only called me by my first name but remembered that we had met years before when they were playing Wembley. I wanted to pick him up and hug him.

As we waited, he asked me where in Wales I was from. To make life easier for him, I just said I was living in Cardiff. I really didn't want to give him a long boring rundown of Cwmaman – not at that moment, anyway.

'Oh,' he said. 'Is the Top Rank still there?'

I was shocked yet again. Apparently, they had played in the Top Rank nightclub on Queen Street in Cardiff many years before they were really famous.

'I love the Welsh,' he added, 'great sense of humour.' He then went on to tell me about the night they had played in the Welsh capital. He said he had done the usual routine of shaking his arse to the crowd dressed as a schoolboy when a woman came up to him in the bar after the show and yelled out in front of everyone, 'Hey, love, the show was shit but you've got a lovely tight arse on you.' And she walked off laughing.

He went up to receive his lifetime achievement award and I stood there feeling so proud for him.

It was at another wild *Kerrang!* ceremony that I first hooked up with the infamous Dirty Sanchez crew. Again I was hosting the awards and I clocked them in the crowd, sitting with the Welsh band the Lostprophets. I told the audience, 'I'm in for a great night: the Dirty Sanchez boys are in town.'

I could see by their beaming faces they were over the moon to be mentioned in such prestigious company. Apparently, it was their first big awards ceremony and it was the time just before they were becoming well known throughout the world.

After the formal presentation stuff, Matthew Pritchard, one of the founders of the *Dirty Sanchez* show, came over to say hello and thank me. He was quiet and unassuming.

As the night progressed, we did what the Welsh are famous for: we formed into one big group and proceeded to get hammered. I remember we popped backstage to my dressing room so I could get changed. I was wearing a circus ringmaster's jacket. Pritchard was in pain. He showed me his knob, which was bleeding. I imagined he had been up to his old tricks and had stapled his old boy to the table or some other bizarre stunt. But, in fact, he'd just had a Prince Albert. He had actually pierced his bell end. It wasn't a pretty sight. Later on we all hit the town until dawn.

Later that year, I met up with the boys at Donington Park, where Black Sabbath were playing. I remember walking through the crowd and looking back to see Pritchard setting a Union Flag on fire while it was draped over some guy's back. There was mass chaos. People were pushing and pulling as he slowly made his getaway. I invited them back to the *Kerrang!* rock'n'roll tent. What a bad mistake. There was free beer, pills, shots, the works. At the time I was hoping that I could get a slot presenting on *Kerrang!* radio. I thought my chances were shot when Pritchard started swinging from the light shade, until it crashed to the floor. Then he tipped a large table full of drinks over on its side. Dan Joyce, the sole English member of the Sanchez gang, was eating horse manure and abusing everyone. We all got banned. I always wonder how the hell someone could get banned from a rock'n'roll tent for being too rock'n'roll.

Pritchard and I became big buddies after that and started to hang out together. He was from Cardiff, and he was just the type of friend I needed at that time. He became my guardian angel, an angel with a big, evil grin, dyed peroxide hair and insanity running through his veins.

As luck would have it, around that time a new bar opened in the capital called the Soda Bar. The owner, Tim, loved the idea of celebrities milling around the club. It was good for its image and he encouraged us to come there often. He treated us like royalty, the full red-carpet treatment. It became our own little version of Studio 54 in New York. At weekends there were queues of people halfway down the street waiting to get in, but we had a VIP entrance and, more importantly, our own cove up near the back. Nothing was too hot or too heavy in the cove.

I felt like a pirate when I was there. Our motto was, 'What goes on in the cove, stays in the cove.'

Some nights all our drinks were free. Jack Daniel's on ice was my favourite tipple at the time. There were always stacks of pills, powder and women everywhere I looked to tempt us. And there was always someone more than happy to offer us a sample of something, which Pritchard and I were more than willing to give a go.

Pritch is quite reserved when you first meet him, but when he gets comfortable in your company he's exactly as he is on *Dirty Sanchez*, wild and unpredictable. He's a real party animal. If I popped a pill, he would pop two. If I drank a bottle of whisky, he'd drink three. If I was the prince of partying, Pritchard was not only the king of overload, he was also the queen, the jack and all the rest of the cards in the pack. He was nonstop and I loved it. It was a mental time and a great laugh. I know this sounds stupid, but some nights the partying lasted three days. It was full-on excess. I was living the rock'n'roll lifestyle to the limit again without a rock'n'roll band.

We would try anything. One of my favourites was a little purple star tablet. It was a mix of LSD and ecstasy. They were so good I had one tattooed on my hand. But they were strong. One night Pritchard gave two to a friend of mine. Twenty minutes later, this boy was on the floor, sweating, hallucinating that he was on fire. We had to surround him and pretend to fan out imaginary flames.

All that partying took its toll and I became a Soda Bar vampire, seeing daylight only during the taxi ride home. Once back in my flat, I rarely opened the curtains to let the sun into my room. I would sleep all day and go out in search of excitement at night, every night.

During some heavy drinking sessions in the Soda Bar, which inevitably stretched out into the early hours of the mornings, Tim, the owner, would throw us the keys and tell us to lock up after we left. After one early-morning session, one of our mates drove us home. He was smashed himself and could hardly stand, let alone drive. As we travelled up one of the streets by my flat, he crashed into a parked car. We got out and surveyed the damage. The owner of the car rushed out, took one look at us and ran back in. We weren't sure if he was going to phone the police or get a gun; we got back in the car and shot away as fast as we could.

Another night in the bar, I was deep in conversion with this rather attractive girl. She was stunning, with long black hair and green eyes. We talked for ages. Anyway, Pritchard was bouncing about playing fuck as normal. I don't think he liked the fact that I was not part of his 'tug' team, especially when we were in the cove. He thought I should be the unofficial fifth member of the Sanchez team.

I was just about to ask the girl if she wanted to come back to my flat with me, when I was whacked on the back of the head with a plastic chair. I landed on the floor. Dazed and shocked, I looked up at a grinning Pritchard.

'What are you doing, you daft bastard?' I cried out.

'Sorry, did I hit you too hard?' he seemed genuinely concerned for me.

'You didn't have to hit me at all.'

'You were asking for it. Go on, you can hit me now.' He held out the chair.

When I returned to my senses, the girl had disappeared. I looked at Pritch. He smiled, and like an old mate, I forgave him and we carried on drinking.

One of the maddest things I remember was the night we went to see Motörhead in Cardiff. After the gig we took their guitarist, Phil Campbell, back to our local. Phil was like the rock'n'roll equivalent of the candy man. He had a black bag like the one a doctor would carry, and when he opened it up, it was full of some of the most rock'n'roll things you could imagine; I'm sure I even saw some Lemsip in there. I knew it was going to be a good night.

We were in the cove, and he was telling me a story about how some rock stars used to take their cocaine. Apparently, there were some stars who had taken so much cocaine in their lives that their noses were knackered and the only way they could get their daily fill of the drug was through a straw up their arse. The hearsay was that one group used to get a roadie to do it for them.

I thought, 'What a weird job!' 'What do you do for a living?' 'Oh, me? I'm a cocaine-up-the-arse-with-a-straw technician.'

It's such a great story; I hope it's true.

A while later Pritchard appeared out of the bog, carrying a plastic beer crate and a piece of string. He dropped his trousers, and got up on the table. 'Stu, Stu!' We all stared at him. He continued, 'Stu, do us a favour. Tie this to the crate and my Prince Albert.'

Phil was in fits of laughter.

'No way,' I replied.

'Come on, I wanna see if I can pick this up with my cock ring.'

'Don't be so stupid, Pritch.'

He turned back to face me. 'And I thought you were fucking rock'n'roll, man.'

'Right, pass it here.'

He handed it to me and there I was, string in mouth, trying to thread it through the ring in his bell-end.

'Hurry up,' he joked.

I laughed so much I was nearly sick.

'Quick, quick! There are people watching.'

Phil was doubled up with laughter. I delicately inserted the string and tied it. It was too weird for words. I have always tried to help my mates out in any way I can – picking them up in my car if they needed a ride or lending them money when they were broke – but this was a new one on me.

Thank fuck the Internet wasn't big at that time, or I bet some bastard would have posted it on YouTube: *'Click here to see a rock star attaching a beer crate with a piece of string to some nutcase's penis.'*

He then proceeded to try to pick up the crate with the ring in his knob. He told us to put beer bottles and stuff into the slots of the crate to add weight. We were laughing like fools, watching him on the table with the crate swinging from his old boy, when suddenly the ring ripped out of his foreskin. There was blood everywhere. 'Fucking hell!' he yelled out and disappeared to another part of the room. Phil's jaw hit the table. Pritchard came back a while later, knob bandaged up and ready to party.

Another bizarre occasion was the night in the club when Charlotte Church and her mother were there. It was Charlotte's birthday and there were lots of press people outside hoping to get some snaps of her leaving legless, or better still, being carried. The press had been hounding the singer at the time and were looking for any scandal they could find about her private life.

When they were about to leave, her mother came over to me and asked if I would mind walking Charlotte out and getting photographed by the paparazzi. Apparently, it wasn't cool to leave a nightclub on your birthday alone, or with your mother.

To be honest, I didn't need the attention at the time. I wanted to keep a low profile, so I suggested that a good friend of mine, Mr Pritchard, would be glad to do it. Of course, he was mad for it. So the odd couple hitched up and walked out of the front doors, hand in hand.

Pritchard told me later it was absolutely mental. It was like walking into a rave with all the flashing lights from the cameras. He joked that he didn't know if he should walk on with her, or take his top off and dance. They got in a taxi, drove around the corner and then he got out and headed back to the club, from where the press had already fucked off.

The next day, their photos were splashed all over the tabloids: CHARLOTTE'S NEW BOYFRIEND; THE NEW LOVE OF CHURCH'S LIFE.

Pritchard's mother was overjoyed. She really thought he would be marrying into millions. He said she was devastated when he told her the truth.

I could imagine sitting in the church listening to the priest on the day of that wedding: 'Charlotte, do you take this fucking psychopath, who staples his knob to a table for kicks, to be your lawful wedded husband?'

For days after, reporters were hiding in the bushes outside his house and rifling through the bins for something to print in their rags. At one stage he said he was going to hide in the bin and jump out and frighten the fuckers to death. Now that would have been a great story!

At another launch party – this one for XFM in the Pop Factory in Porth – it soon became apparent, even to me, that I was getting out of control. Things were becoming too berserk, even for me. I was sitting on a table snorting coke through a straw straight out of the bag, and no, I never was tempted to do it up the arse. It was strong stuff and it really hit me hard. I couldn't speak, my nose was running. Pritchard and the rest of the Dirty Sanchez boys were being presented a Rock-and-Roll Excess award. On stage Pritchard took the mike and said, 'Anyway, thanks for the award, but if anyone deserves it more than us it's Stuart Cable – he's right off it, full excess.' He pointed at me. Everyone turned to stare. I sat frozen like a rabbit in headlights; I couldn't even smile. At that moment, I knew I had to do something about my lifestyle, and soon. I knew I was on the slippery slope to nowhere.

But I had a great time with Matthew Pritchard. Years later I remember when I was giving an interview to the *Wales on Sunday* newspaper and I jokingly said I was leaving the bright lights of Cardiff and moving back to my old village because I wanted to get away from Pritchard from Dirty Sanchez, because if I didn't, I would probably end up dead or round the bend – or both.

He told me afterwards it was the nicest thing anyone had ever said about him. But he was, and still is, a great mate.

During that last year and a half in the bright lights of Cardiff I met a girl called Sarah Morgan. I wasn't really looking for someone; I was still secretly grieving for Lisa. I was introduced to her by Swampy, my old drum tech, when I mentioned I was looking to put a band together. By now, I was starting to get itchy drumstick fingers and wanted music back in my life. He told me he knew this gorgeous bass guitarist. She sounded perfect.

We met up and had a couple of jams together. She was an extremely talented guitarist and very attractive. She loved rock'n'roll music and looked very much rock'n'roll: six foot tall, black T-shirts, short punky blonde hair – and with the attitude to match. We had a lot in common as far as music was concerned. She also loved the Who, AC/DC and Floyd. We started to date, and not long afterwards, she moved in with me.

Sarah was a great woman to have around, although I knew she wasn't everyone's cup of tea. She could be quite outspoken at times and would often make situations kind of awkward for people. But she was a great thinker and communicator. She could talk to most people about most subjects; she always had an opinion and wasn't shy in coming forward to let people know what was on her mind.

When we first started to go to parties together where people didn't know her, she would tell them she used to be a hooker. At one arty-farty party, she told a guy about her previous 'occupation'. Later on he came over to me and said, 'Stu, do you mind if I ask you a question?'

'Yes,' I stared at him, 'her name *is* Mabel Cable, okay?'

The bloke shook his head. 'No, do you know the girl you're with used to be a prostitute?' I felt like Richard Gere from the film *Pretty Woman*.

She was wild like that, though, didn't care a toss what people thought. Sarah was the one who actually told me to phone Kelly the night that 'Dakota' went to Number 1 in the British charts. We were sitting in my flat after a night of heavy partying and she could tell I was depressed. I had heard the song on MTV and had a feeling it was going to do well. When I was in the band, there were many singles that I thought would get us that coveted Number 1 slot, but it never happened while I was part of it all, and I just didn't want to deal with 'Dakota' getting there.

'Go on,' she told me, 'phone Kelly and tell him well done.'

'Fuck off!' was my first reaction.

'You'll be the bigger man for it. He won't expect it from you and he'll hate it, trust me.'

I still wasn't convinced it was the right thing to do, but I went along with it, even though it was killing me inside. I called him to congratulate him and I was really glad I did. It did make me feel better.

Sarah slotted quite comfortably into my insane type of lifestyle. We had a ball together. Lisa and I knew how to party, but with Sarah things went to a new level; she became a 24-hour party person right alongside me. She used to come to the Soda Bar with me and the rest of the gang. She wanted the excitement, the wild times, the all-night benders; she became a vampire like me. I remember her taping black bin bags to the windows of my flat to blacken out the room. My living room was just a mass of pillows, and cushions on the floor and people crashing out. Our lifestyle meant that weekends were just a blur.

But Sarah was also very driven and focused when it came to my future. She challenged me to step back up to the plate, to get back to where I had come from. She was always pushing me, and I liked her for that. We stayed together for a while, but deep down I knew it wasn't going to work out between us. There had been many nights when I woke up beside her and thought she was Lisa. It was confusing for me and completely unfair on her.

I had some other issues around the corner at that time too. I hadn't yet got my settlement from the band, and money was getting tight. I used to wake up in the middle of the night in a cold sweat. I had nightmares about returning to the life before I had become successful, back to delivering school dinners, or working on that fly press, or, worse still, signing on the dole. Even to this day, it scares me to think of being skint. I find myself scrutinising every bill that comes in, wondering how long before I won't be able to afford to live the lifestyle I have become accustomed to, even though my financial advisers keep telling me I haven't got anything to worry about, as long as I don't go mad and buy several hundred signed rugby shirts.

The settlement money from the Stereophonics split eventually did arrive, and this time I was going to make sure no one took that off me, as they had done with the band.

I decided to leave Cardiff and go back to home to Aberdare. I went back to stay with Nicola without telling Sarah. She was upset and took it hard at first.

I tried to forget about the last few years and just be a normal father and some kind of husband again. It was okay at first. I felt as though I had just awoken from a coma that I had been in for about a year and a half and I could see the light, smell the flowers again, all that bullshit.

But after about four months the doubt kicked in again. I know this will sound terrible, but I did try to love Nicola again; I wanted it to be the way it used to be. But it wasn't. I will always love her for being the mother of my child, and we did have some great times together. I would never want to see any harm come to her in a million years, but realistically, I was still searching for the 'Lisa Rogers' girl and it was eating at my brain.

It become obvious to me I was living a sham and it was wrong and unfair, especially on Nicola and Cian. Then one day the reality police came knocking on my door in the shape of Nicola's mother.

'I want you to move out,' she told me quite forcefully.

'Pardon me?' Her aggression had stunned me for a minute.

'You heard me. I want you to move out.'

I fought back. 'You don't speak to me like that in my house, the house I paid for, and the house your daughter lives in.'

She didn't flinch. 'Don't you understand? I want you to get out now, today. You've ruined my daughter's life as it is, and I don't want you to ruin it any more.'

Her words hit me across the face like a right hook from Mike Tyson. I didn't have the right words inside me to make a counterargument: I felt like a wounded dog no one cared about, who had been left to die by the side of the road. I couldn't believe I was being driven out of my own house, but deep down I knew she was right and I went upstairs and packed my bag.

Nicola didn't deserve any of this, didn't deserve what I had become. As a matter of fact our divorce papers had just come through around this time. So I bought a house about a mile away – believe it or not, in another posh part of Aberdare – acquired two dogs and began leading a 'normal life' not far from my boy.

'I've always been a very big fan of the Stereophonics and will never forget the big gig they did in Swansea with 50,000 fans. I couldn't go to it because of work, but I bought the video of it and remember it giving me goose bumps all over my body. The Welshness of it all was amazing and I always remember seeing Stuart playing the drums with the "I'm loving this moment" expression written all over his face. He had rock'n'roll written all over him.

'I remember thinking, "I bet he's a right laugh on the piss." So you could imagine what I was like the first opportunity I had to meet him at the *Kerrang!* Awards he was hosting in London. I'll never forget when he first got on the stage and mentioned he was in the good company of the Dirty Sanchez boys, which made the four of us so stoked. Because of what we do, people love to stay well away from us, let alone mention us, but Cable mentioned us with pride. Thank you, butt.

'Ever since that night, I became good friends with him and we had many a good smash-up in Cardiff. Stuart is an amazing bloke. There are so many ways to explain his character/personality. He's one of those people that you'll never have a dull moment with, who knocks out quotes every five minutes and is louder than a Flat Holm Island foghorn. He's never grumpy, always happy, and has a brain that could tell you more rock'n'roll stories than Mötley Crüe's book, *The Dirt*. On that note, *Demons and Cocktails* is Stuart's dirt.'

**Matthew Pritchard, founder member of Dirty Sanchez**

# CHAPTER 12

# WE HAVE THE HAIR PRODUCTS, WE CAN REBUILD HIM

I didn't know where I was going, or what the hell I was going to do, but I packed up, got in my car and left for good. Keith Richards sprang to mind again. I wondered what he would do in my position. I drove aimlessly about, thinking that it would be nice to have someone to talk to, someone who could give me some good sound advice. As if my guardian angel had heard me, my phone rang. On the other end was Dewi Morris, or Dewi Puss to his mates. Dewi had starred in the 1978 iconic one-off Welsh TV comedy *Grand Slam* and had recently become a good friend and mentor. I was delighted to answer the phone.

He had called me up, on the off chance to see what I was doing. Maybe he had sensed my situation.

'I'm driving about. Fancy a drink?' I asked, hoping he would say yes.

'Hark, hark the lark. I would love a pint of dark in Cardiff Arms

Park,' he said. 'Meet me in my local in Whitchurch in an hour.' He sounded as manic as ever.

I had got to know Dewi really well several weeks before when we were paired up on the BBC Wales programme *The Big Welsh Challenge*. It was a linguistic challenge in which five non-Welsh-speaking celebrities had several weeks to master the Welsh language, with the help of five celebrities who already spoke it fluently.

Dewi was my mentor. I wasn't sure if he knew what he had got himself into. To be honest, I was actually looking forward to it. My son was going to a Welsh-speaking school, so I thought it would be a great opportunity for me to learn and help him, or probably for him to help me.

The first day I met up with Dewi, we went to the BBC to try and understand more about the format for the programme. We walked into the canteen, and the place was packed. I think the entire cast of the popular S4C Welsh-language soap *Pobol y Cwm* were there munching away.

'What do you want to eat?' he asked, handing me a tray.

'Whatever's here, you prick,' I joked.

He smirked in a kind of 'Oh, okay, it's going to be like that, is it?' kind of way. Little did I know, he would have his revenge.

We got some grub, but before we sat down, he piped up, 'Excuse me, everyone.'

I could feel the colour draining away from my cheeks; I just knew he was going to embarrass me. 'Everyone, my new butty here, Stuart Cable, is coming out of the closet today.' Everyone looked at me, fork frozen in mid-air. He added, 'He would just like you all to know that, as from today, he is now officially gay. So let's give him a big round of applause.'

# WE HAVE THE HAIR PRODUCTS, WE CAN REBUILD HIM

I went beetroot. Unbelievably they all started clapping. A few people actually stood up. 'And also' – unfortunately, he wasn't finished: he pointed towards some guy in the corner, eating a plate of chips – 'he also told me he fancied that guy over there.'

First, I wanted to kill him and then I wanted the ground to open up and swallow me whole. But, as I soon found out, this was just his sense of humour and he has the type of personality that lets him get away with it. He even took my new 'gayness' one step further by putting up posters in the window of his house stating the fact that Stuart Cable was gay and proud of it.

But Dewi was serious when it came to teaching me all the Welsh stuff. 'You will fucking learn it, Stuart Cable! You are Welsh and if you don't learn it, I will tell everyone you were thrown out of the band for liking disco music.'

The whole experience started out as a nightmare. As part of the challenge we had to stay in a communal house in North Wales for a week. It was like some prison camp positioned in an old slate mine. The place was scary. It reminded me of a spooky hotel where, once upon a time, the innkeeper had brutally murdered the guests, one by one, and stashed them under the floorboards.

My room was like a poor excuse for a youth hostel. The worst part was, there was no television.

'Where's my TV?' I asked the woman who had shown me to my room.

'You are here to learn this week, Stuart, not to watch television.'

I thought, 'Fucking great! I've been inducted into the Welsh version of the fucking Moonies.'

By the next day I had already cracked. I needed to escape before I strangled someone or beat them to death with my textbook.

227

# DEMONS AND COCKTAILS

I felt like Jack Nicholson's character in *The Shining*. All Welsh and no TV makes Stuart a dull boy. Or, if I had actually been listening while in the class, that would now read, '*Popeth Cymraeg a dim teledu yn troi Stuart mewn i fachgen diflas.*'

Thankfully, for all concerned, Dewi was working in a village about ten miles away. I called him up. 'Dewi, you have got to get me out of here. I'm going nuts.'

'Meet me at the village pub,' he offered.

So, under the cover of darkness, instead of doing homework that was due in the morning, I ordered a taxi and headed out to see Dewi and to get pissed in the pub. He introduced me to all the locals. He told them I was there for the competition and instructed them to speak to me only in Welsh.

I thought, 'Fucking hell! I can't get away from it.'

One guy came over and said something to me. The only bit I could make out was the word Stereophonics.

I shook my head. 'Sorry, mate, I haven't learnt that bit yet.'

Dewi roared with laughter. Everyone else joined in. And that was more or less how it went each night. They tried their best to communicate with me, but not knowing what the hell they were on about, I just shrugged and carried on as if I did. I had a great time. One night, though, I thought I was going to get my lights knocked out by some big bruiser when his rather friendly girlfriend took a shine to me. But he turned out to be a really nice guy, if not a little naïve when it came to his choice of girlfriend.

Back in the prison camp, things went from bad to worse. I ended up making some girl in the class cry for having a go at my 'lack of commitment'. I thought, 'Who the fuck do you think you are? Kelly bloody Jones?' I gave her a mouthful and stormed out like a prima donna having a bad-hair day.

I felt bad later, but the whole thing reminded me of school and it just switched me off totally. But I did learn some Welsh by the end of the show, and more importantly, Dewi and I became great mates.

So, after the phone call, I met up with him in his local pub in Whitchurch, Cardiff. Over a few beers, I explained to him what was going on in my life, the mess I was in, and everything else I could think of that I needed to get off my chest. It felt good just to sit and talk.

'Where are you going to go?' he asked, concerned for me.

'I'm going to book into some hotel to sort my head out for a while, then who knows?' I really hadn't thought that far ahead.

He looked a little cross. 'No way, you are not going to some hotel. You're coming home with me. I don't want any arguments, Cable boy.'

I knew we were both slightly drunk and that he would probably regret it in the morning, but I was over the moon he had asked me. And home I went, to stay with him and his wonderful wife, Rhiannon. As we walked through the door, I remember him saying, 'Oh, before you go in my living room, you wash your fucking feet.' I stopped in my tracks. He burst out laughing.

I stayed for six months, and no exaggeration, it was the best six months of my life. We spent many a long drunken night, sitting in front of the fire, laughing, eating and doing a lot of *siarad*-ing, which for the non-Welsh speakers out there doesn't mean anything rude: *siarad* is Welsh for talk. They both liked to *siarad*.

We talked about everything and anything. They helped me turn myself around: I started playing golf again, going to nice restaurants and learning to appreciate a proper red wine.

He taught me to sing the Welsh National Anthem while we sat in his living room, with my feet washed and fresh.

I could see the pride in him and Rhiannon when I sang it, word perfect – well, *nearly* word perfect. And I was glad that he made me learn it. I think every Welsh person should learn the Welsh National Anthem and, more importantly, they should be proud to sing it. We have been more than happy as a Welsh nation to let go of our identity, of our language, and to let our heritage just saunter away into obscurity.

Dewi was always taking the piss. One day while in the pub he rushed in panting. Everyone stopped to listen. 'Stu,' he said, 'there's a band I know who have got a few gigs lined up, but they haven't got a drummer.' He left a pause.

I was thinking to myself, 'I wouldn't mind a spot of drumming. It's been a while now.'

Then he added, 'I was wondering if you knew of any good drummers about. What about that Argentinian guy who plays with your old mates?' He burst out laughing and the rest of the pub followed suit. He had done me like a kipper yet again!

I think I would have stayed with Dewi and Rhiannon until I was old and grey if they hadn't decided to sell up and move back to North Wales. Dewi is the funniest and wittiest man I have ever known in my life, and the most entertaining. Rhiannon is a perfect match for his madness and she is a lovely, lovely woman. They really helped me to get my act back together; they cared about me more in that short space of time than anyone has ever cared about me in my entire life. They were my North Walian mother and father. I actually called them Mam and Dad from time to time.

Dewi was like the father I had so cruelly lost all those years before. I'm not ashamed to say I will cry a billion sobs the day he dies. I would be more than happy to carry his coffin, all by myself, a thousand miles over hot coals, if need be. I love them both to death.

Before we parted company, Dewi had a long serious chat with me about my future. There were no jokes, no piss-taking. He told me he cared about me and lectured me about keeping my life together, especially after I had come so far in the last six months. With his words ringing in my ears, I decided it was time to go back home.

I knew it wouldn't work out if I tried to move back in with Nicola again, so, as I mentioned before, I decided to buy a nice house in Aberdare, not too far from her and Cian. I wanted to spend time with my boy and try to get things back to normal.

Settling back into Valleys life was actually a very smooth transition for me. Unlike Richard and Kelly, who had left for the bright city lights, pretty girls and 24/7 traffic, I had always lived more or less in or around the area, so I didn't have to rebuild relationships with people in town. I had always stayed close to my circle of friends. Even at the height of the band's fame, I made a point of going out and having a few beers with my mates or popping down the local to say hello to people.

I really began to enjoy life in a completely different way: relaxing, riding my Harley or just sitting in my local, the Welsh

Harp, and talking. It was nice to be back in my home town, where I could go out with my mates and not have to worry about trouble, not have to be concerned someone taking the piss in a threatening way or trying to make a name for themselves by giving me a dig. It was nice to live a life where the worst of my behaviour consisted of getting drunk in the pub and inviting everyone back to my house and making them sit through my Who and AC/DC DVDs.

It was like being on the dole but with no money problems. I just needed to get some purpose and structure in my life. I started to watch and play sport again, too, which I hadn't done for ages. I became a member of a golf club and started playing five-a-side football with the boys, which I still do today. When I was feeling super-brave, I even went for a jog now and then, but never too far.

I had forgotten how exciting live sport was, and how much I enjoyed watching it and hanging out with the players. I began to reacquaint myself with some of the sports stars I had met while I was in the band. One of them was one of the best rugby players the world has ever seen, Jonathan Davies. Jonathan had invited me to his wedding a few years before. He was marrying a lovely girl called Helen. It was a big posh affair covered by *OK!* magazine. It wasn't the typical cheap-plonk-and-sausage-roll buffet I had grown up with.

On the day, I sat on a table with Max Boyce, whom I had met before. He had the entire table in stitches all day, story after story, joke after joke. Towards the end of the night, everyone was drunk. I was up on the tables dancing like a mad fool with Jonathan, Alan Bateman, Ieuan Evans and another famous boy from my own town, Dai Young, who was coaching Cardiff's rugby team.

## WE HAVE THE HAIR PRODUCTS, WE CAN REBUILD HIM

Jonathan and I were on the same table at opposite ends. I am the worst dancer in the world, so I must have looked a right odd sight jiving away. Everything was going great guns, until Jonathan for some reason decided to join me on my side of the table. You don't have to be a brain surgeon to know what happened next. It had disaster written all over it. The one end of the table shot up in the air, quickly followed by Jonathan and me, who fell to the floor. Jonathan, being a nimble-footed ex-player, employed all his rugby survival instincts and somehow managed to use me as a human cushion. I hit the floor and he landed right on top of me. I thought it was the least I could do for him on his wedding night. The music stopped and everyone looked at the chaos we had caused.

Then the laughter erupted. When I got to my feet, Jonathan noticed that I had sliced my arse on a wineglass. There was blood pissing down my ripped trouser leg. It looked as if I needed a stitch or two. I didn't know if I should go to the hospital and get treatment, or stay and enjoy the rest of the night. In the end, it wasn't really much of a decision to a recovering former party animal like me: I legged it upstairs, covered the wound with a serviette and rejoined the dancing with a big rip in my trousers and blood streaming into my socks. What a night to remember!

Jonathan later invited me to his testimonial dinner at the Grosvenor Hotel in London. I was honoured to say the least. On the journey by train to the event, I met up with another rugby legend, Scott Gibbs. We sat together and hit it off straightaway. I had bumped into him a few times before, while I was in the band, but I really got to know him on the three-hour train ride. After a couple of gin and tonics, we found out that we shared a passion for the group Rush. I was in my oils as we discussed song after song, album after album, in great detail. I also discovered that Scott had actually dreamt of being a drummer like his father, which was really strange because I had always wanted to be a rugby player like *my* father. I became a good mate of Scott's and we went to see Rush many times together after that day.

When we got to the Grosvenor Hotel, we couldn't believe that it was as posh as fuck. It was a five-star black-tie job, polished shoes, the full works. At one point I thought I was at the Sports Personality of the Year Awards. It was wall-to-wall superstars. I was sitting on the same table with rugby royalty in the intimidating shapes of *the* Martin Johnston, World Cup winner Sean Fitzpatrick and ex-All Blacks captain and Rugby League superstar Shane Edwards. I felt rather intimidated as I sat among them, feeling like a little pot-bellied drummer boy perched on the shoulders of rugby giants.

But of course they were a great bunch of guys, your typical down-to-earth set of rugby boys. After the formal bit with all the speeches and the stories about Jonathan's life, both on and off the field, the fun really started.

Jonathan came rushing over to me and asked me to go up on stage and start off the karaoke.

'Jon, I'm a drummer, remember?'

'Come on, Stu, just for me.' He looked at me with his puppy-dog eyes.

I couldn't resist the limelight. So up on stage I trotted, the haunting memory of my one night of singing with Nail Bomb playing out in my mind. I looked at all the people staring back at me. 'Bloody hell!' I thought. 'This is worse than stepping out at Glastonbury.'

Jonathan was at the side of the stage, giggling like a schoolboy. For some reason I decided to sing 'Born to be Wild'. I got through the first verse without much of a problem. Everyone sat there smiling politely, *too* politely. I took the mike out of the stand, marched to the front and screamed, 'Come on, you motherfuckers, sing!' I had learnt the trick at a recent Metallica concert I had attended.

Jonathan dropped his head into his hands, but it did the trick: soon everyone was up on their feet, singing. Maybe *I* should have been the frontman all along, instead of Kelly!

When I got back to the table, Sean Fitzpatrick told me it was the funniest thing he had ever seen in his life. During the rest of the night we all got completely annihilated.

At this point, I also became friendly with another sporting superstar in the form of the world champion snooker player, Mark Williams. I met him at some function in Cardiff and spent all night talking to him about the game and how he played certain shots. I had always been a huge snooker fan. Obviously, my father's great passion had rubbed off on me.

Mark invited me back to his home. We were having a few drinks and he was showing me some trick shots and how to screw the ball back properly. I was a little apprehensive about ripping the cloth.

'Don't worry, Stu, nothing will rip this cloth,' he assured me.

We played a game, and, believe it or not, I was whooping him big time. I was up by 31 points with only 27 left on the table. Only the colours were left, which meant that not only would he need to pot them all, but he would also have to snooker me and make me miss one shot. I was waltzing around the room, smug as fuck, holding my cue. There I was, beating a world champion at his own sport, in his own fucking backyard. I only wished that Julian could have been there to take a photo of me racing around the table with my shirt over my head like a footballer celebrating after scoring a goal, when I finally beat the great Mark Williams.

'You ain't going to live this down,' I mocked him. 'You've won the World Championship twice and this numpty from Cwmaman is going to whip you.'

I could see his expression change. At one point I thought he was going to whack me over the head with his cue. He knew he would never live it down if I won; he knew I would shout my victory from the rooftops. Mark lined up a shot, potted the yellow and incredibly ripped the cloth right down the middle!

'We can't play on now,' he said.

'You fucking done that on purpose!' I yelled at him.

'Honest to God, I didn't.' He just smiled and put the cues away, along with my big claim to fame of beating the world champion snooker player.

In the spring of 2004 my radio career was born. The world of radio came along like a white knight on a big Arab charger when Maggie Russell, head of talent at BBC Wales, suggested that I approach the head of BBC Radio Wales about doing a radio show. My meeting with the guy led to my radio show *Cable Rock*, a classic rock radio show on Monday evenings from seven to eight o'clock. The show filled the void left in my life since the split with the band. It was perfect: talking, playing music, everything I loved. It was nerve-racking to begin with, though. I used to script what I was going to say, work it out in detail, but then I just relaxed and grew into the role. It suited me down to the ground.

A year or so later, John Brand, who was still my agent, got a phone call from Kerrang! radio. They had heard what I was doing, and wondered if I was interested in doing a Friday night and Sunday show for them. I did both shows until Cable Rock finished in 2007.

Kerrang! was a lot more controlling as far as what I was allowed to play was concerned, but I didn't really mind because it was a lot of fun, quite different from the rock show, but also it paid a lot more money. Again it was nerve-racking, but my producer on the show, Loz Guest, was absolutely brilliant and helped me tremendously in the beginning.

On my first day with Kerrang!, I co-hosted with Caroline Beavon. We were doing a feature called 'Fist Full of Legends', where we asked listeners to name their top three classic-rock tracks and why they liked them. We were live on air talking to this guy in Scotland. Of course his name just happened to be Jimmy. I asked him what he thought of the show so far.

'I think it's fucking great, Stu.'

'Thanks, Jim, but you can't swear on live radio.'

He was apologetic, but did the same in his next sentence. In the end I had to cut him short.

After the show I had a call from the boss.

I thought, 'Shit, it's over before it's started.'

But he was cool about it. He realised it wasn't my fault.

I still co-host on Kerrang! with Caroline. Performing with her is great. It's nice to have someone to bounce things off, someone who understands my personality and what makes me tick. It really helps me find the funny moments without trying to be funny; it's good being part of a double act, the Morecambe and Wise type of approach. I also think the listening audience appreciates it too – not having to put up with me droning on and on.

In 2007 another radio opportunity came along. Nick Davidson, head of Cardiff's Red Dragon radio, left to help set up XFM in South Wales. He approached me about hosting the breakfast show. I did consider it, but knew that it would completely mess up my social life, and I've never been the best at getting up in the mornings, anyway. I told Nick I would love to be part of the station but maybe something more suited to my lifestyle. So I got the Saturday show. It was great while it lasted. There were also a host of other celebrities presenting during the week, such as my old mates, Pritchard and Dainton from Dirty Sanchez. But, for whatever reason, it didn't work out and the station finished after only six months on air, which was a real shame.

As with my TV career, I think I really got better and better on the radio as time went on. It's all about learning by your mistakes and not making them again. I've learnt how to handle the things that used to throw me off like a seasoned pro. I remember introducing a song by the Kaiser Chiefs when I first started, and there was complete silence. I panicked a bit and broke the golden rule of radio and muttered to myself on air, 'Fucking hell!' Nowadays I've learnt to handle dead air and not be afraid of it.

Although I was enjoying the radio career very much, the

drummer in me was dying to dust down his old drumsticks and get back out and play. I needed the thrill again of having my music aired on the radio, not just playing other bands' stuff. My passion for music had subconsciously been locked away in a little room in my mind after the split; now it was time to set it free. I hooked up with two brothers, Andy and Steve Williams, who played lead guitar and bass respectively. Next, Richie King joined on rhythm. A while later, I came across a great vocalist, Greg Jones, who coincidentally is from Cwmaman. I met him while I was doing some TV work to find local talent.

We named the band Killing for Company, after a book based on the life of serial killer Dennis Nilsen, and no, we didn't get the inspiration from KFC (Kentucky Fried Chicken). We weren't that finger-lickin' clever!

Jamming with the boys was a pleasure, a breath of fresh air. It was great having no egos in the room, except for maybe the drummer's, and it felt terrific to start to create new material again. Greg was the main wordsmith while the rest of us had a hand in the music. It's a very different type of music from that of the 'Phonics: more rock, a lot heavier.

When we started out, I think my name closed a few doors for us on the music scene, but, on the other hand, it also opened many as well. When I found out the Who were playing in Swansea, I emailed Roger Daltrey to ask if there was any chance of our getting on the bill. I sent him out a few of our songs to see what he thought.

I also phoned Scott Gibbs, who I knew was working for the Liberty Stadium in Swansea itself. He thought I wanted some free tickets, so he was quite surprised when I told him, 'No, Scott, you don't understand. I want to fucking play with my new band.' He said he would see what he could do, and fair play to him, he got in touch with the promoters immediately.

A few days later, I had an email from Roger telling me he loved the material and the Who wanted us to support them. If only everything in life were that simple!

The show went very well for us. It was a great experience. Standing stage-side and watching the Who play their set brought back memories of the time the 'Phonics had supported them in Earl's Court. There were a lot of Stereophonics fans there to see what my new band was like. Hopefully they liked what they saw and we picked up a few new fans.

My celebrity popularity was starting to grow a bit, especially in and around Wales. I was asked to attend awards ceremonies, present awards, go to gala dinners and do lots of charity events; everyone seemed to want a piece of me. It had all started a few years earlier, when I was asked to do one of the strangest, but most rewarding things I have ever done: front up a national billboard campaign under the banner, BLLCKS. It was to raise awareness of testicular cancer among young males. They were looking for someone who would appeal to the younger generation of the Welsh. I didn't have to think twice; I have always tried to help as many people or organisations as possible. To be honest, most people think it's one of those things that only happens to someone else. I remember the first time I checked myself. It was strange, like feeling two walnuts in a sock. It really heightened my own awareness. The publicity was great: me with my hand on my crotch with the slogan, 'Do yourself a favour, check yourself while you've still got the balls.' Simple, but extremely powerful.

I'll never forget the day I was walking through the streets in Cardiff and saw myself on massive posters, billboards, backs of buses, everywhere. I thought, 'Fucking hell! This is nuts.' No pun intended. But it is such a deadly subject, and no laughing matter, so I was more than willing to help and to give my support.

And hopefully it worked. I was called up by a woman who thanked me because her son had seen the advert and checked himself only to find a lump. Unfortunately he lost his scrotum, but he was still alive and doing well.

'What I love about Stu is the fact he is always full of life and always very positive. Everyone can relate to him and he's got this captivating quality about him, which lights up a room. It doesn't matter if you have only talked to him for five minutes or five hours, you know that by the end of the conversation you have meet someone really special. He truly is the quintessential Welshman and a great ambassador for the country. Stuart is the last of the big-time drummers. And, on top of all that, he is also a massive Rush fan.'

**Scott Gibbs, rugby superstar and Rush fan**

'The great thing about Stuart is what you see is what you get. He's a loveable, down-to-earth guy who hasn't changed one bit over the years. He is always a bundle of energy and great fun to be around.

'I may not see him for months on end but when I do, I find that he's got this very special gift of making you feel like the most important person in the room.

'I regard him as a very close and special friend.'

**Jonathan Davies, rugby superstar and TV commentator**

'Stuart's God-given ability to talk crap for an extended period of time meant that a career in broadcasting was always within his grasp. It was just a matter of smoothing out the rough bits (which is an ongoing process). However, it's his love for music (albeit mainly Rush and AC/DC) that really shines through, and of course his voice, which sounds like he has swallowed a lump of coal, although the ladies seem to like it.'

**Loz Guest, Producer Kerrang! Radio**

## CHAPTER 13

# LUCKY FOR STU?

So here I am, the last chapter of this part of my life. Trust my luck for it to be number 13! It's taken about six months to get thirty-something fun, sad, stressful, electrifying years out of my head and down on paper. I don't think anyone would disagree that I've not only been there and done it, but got the T-shirt from fucking Topshop to prove it.

I've been very lucky and privileged to have had the opportunity to experience a world others might only dream of. I realised from the start of the book that its content would shock and maybe upset some people. I didn't really set out to do that, so if I have, then I apologise to some degree. But warts and all was what I agreed on when Bunko and I sat down to outline the plan of my life story, and that's what I tried to deliver, no holds barred. So I think it's time to finish this off by sharing my thoughts on life now and in the future.

The group Killing for Company are going well, really well.

We've already headlined several large events, and we have been given the opportunity to support some great bands such as the Who, Status Quo and Mike Peters of the Alarm, to name but a few. We continue to write new material and get better all the time. I'm not naïve enough to believe we are going to rise as quickly up the ladder as the Stereophonics did. I don't expect for one minute there will be another Richard Branson riding in on a big white horse to throw a bag of money and fame at us. We know it will take lots of hard work and a fair share of luck. In the end it's really up to us if we have the balls and the appetite to go for it.

We recently went into a recording studio to do some of our own songs with the top-rated US music producer, Bob Marlette. Bob's been around and has produced some big artists such as Alice Cooper, Black Sabbath and many more. We spent a week together in Monnow Valley Studios in Rockfield, near Monmouth. It was a strange feeling to be back in a studio recording again, especially Monnow Valley, because we had recorded some of the *Performance and Cocktails* album there. I walked around on the second morning, eating cornflakes in my socks and looking at all the photos and the copy of the Stereophonics' gold disc displayed on the wall.

That week with Bob was eventful to say the least. He's a tough taskmaster who really knows his stuff. He not only challenged our material, but also the direction and the image of the band; he bashed us all out of shape a little. He told Greg that he was a wonderful singer but that he looked like an accountant, which I think was unfair because he's got a great stage presence. And he told Steve, on bass, that he was a throwback to the Iron Maiden days – again unfair, but funny. He simply told the rest of us that we needed to improve our playing. I found it hilarious watching Bob stroll around the sound booth, barking out orders and killing flies with a big yellow swatter. Although he was tough, and sometimes contradicted himself during the week, he was honest in his appraisal and it was the kick up the arse we needed. His words really hit home about what we had to do to make it.

I know it's going to be tough, especially with the age of the group, since there are a lot of good up-and-coming bands around. It's going to be a long, hard slog. A big part of me would welcome back the rock'n'roll lifestyle with all its demons and temptations knocking at my door in a heartbeat: the touring, the late nights, the hotel rooms, the crappy dressing rooms, and the living out of a suitcase, but the more sensible half of my brain is yelling out loudly, just to make sure I don't do anything stupid, 'Hey, Cable, you would be fucking nuts to go through all that again.'

The experience with Bob made me think about my future, and where I wanted to be in the next couple of years. It made me wonder if I had already had my fifteen minutes of musical fame when I was with Kelly and Richard. Would the new band take me on a journey like the one I had just stepped off with the Stereophonics? Or would I have to bite the bullet and play drums only for pleasure while I try to carve out a different career? I know I'm heading for that crossroads quite soon. I'm not getting any younger, or prettier. I don't think there will be another band if Killing for Company breaks up, unless I get asked to join some kind of supergroup like Velvet Revolver. But can't see that happening.

Should I just accept that my time has come and gone, and move on in a different direction? I've always said I would love to retire by the time I'm 48 and piss off to live in France. It would be great just to chill out, ride bikes all day, or sit drinking wine. I've made some investments over the last few years, which, if everything stays as they are, will give me a solid foundation.

The next 18 months or so is going to be really important to me. I would love the opportunity to do more TV work; maybe another chat show or a part in a sitcom or film. I'm always being asked to do small cameo roles in Welsh-made productions. Who knows? I could end up being the next Vinnie Jones.

**Stuart Cable stars in the new British blockbuster ...**
*Lock, Stock and Two Smoking Hair Dryers*

No, seriously, TV is one option for me. My radio profession is another. It's where I've got the biggest profile at the moment and it's where people say I should concentrate. At present I'm just scratching away at the surface. To do it more seriously, I would probably have to move to Birmingham or London for a while, but I could cope with that if there was a clear path ahead of me.

My personal life is also coming together quite nicely. I have surrounded myself with a great bunch of my old friends, who look out for me and keep me on the straight and narrow, even though I know I drive them all round the bend on many occasions.

Nicola and I now get on probably better than at any time since we first got married. We are really cool. We even go on holidays together a few times a year with Cian. She's a great mother and we are the best of friends. We help each other out all the time. It's funny how putting two people in a different kind of relationship has worked out so well. She still warns me about returning to my old Peter Pan lifestyle and trying always to be the life and soul of the party, but I will never go back down that road again. My love for my boy will ensure that: he is my guiding light.

And he's such a cool kid. He's a typical, normal but nutty Valleys boy. He's such a joy and pleasure to be with, really funny and quick-witted. He's good at school and his vocabulary is superb. He is very alert and astute, unlike his dad, who has the concentration levels of a newt. Just ask Bunko about the interviews we did together.

Of course, he wants to be a drummer like his old man and, to be fair, he's already quite good – some would say already better than his old man! After all that's happened to me, I think I'll tell him to be a lawyer – that's where all the money is. But he also wants to learn guitar, be a world champion pool player and a darts player. He loves motorbiking and wants to compete in all the races. He wants to be the best at everything, and I don't think there's anything wrong with that.

God knows what the future's got in store for him, but I would never pressurise him into any career. I'll give him advice, share my mistakes and help him in any way I can to get a foothold in whatever career he chooses. Obviously I would love to see him walking out at Glastonbury one day in the future, or running out in the red shirt of Wales. I'd even like to see him do something in the world of the media, unlike kids of my generation, who were never encouraged to follow a role in the arts, or any of that fluffy stuff. In my day it was all about being good at maths and English, and then getting an apprenticeship in some factory or working down the pits. I want him to experience more in life than clocking on from nine to five. I would love him to travel and see the real world, the world outside the Valleys, but I will support him 150 million per cent in whatever he does, even if it's delivering lunches to hungry schoolkids. At the moment I'm enjoying every single minute I can with him and trying to be the father I lost so early in my own life.

As far as the Stereophonics – or the Kelly Jones Quartet as it has now become – are concerned, wherever I go I still get people asking me if I have any regrets about leaving the band. I explain that what happened happened, and it's over. I enjoyed most of it when I was there. There's no use letting things fester, and to be honest, this book has helped dispel a few little demons of mine on that score.

I'm not sure what the future holds for the Stereophonics, but if their record sales are any indication, I don't think it's good. It looks, from where I'm standing, that the band is slowly but surely dying. And of course they still haven't broken America, even after all the slogging from coast to coast. I can imagine Kelly is gutted – that was his dream. But I think it's too late for them to get to that superstar level. People and music have moved on. I'm not sure where they both will end up.

Richard is a quiet guy; he toes the line. He does whatever he's told and he's a bit of a 'yes' man to Kelly. In my opinion the band was always to do with Kelly and me. Richard never did that much to promote us in the early days, never went around putting posters up and things like that. God knows what would happen if the band split up. I can't see him being the type of guy to start a new band, but you never know: stranger things have happened in the weird world of rock music. I haven't really spoken to him much in five years, and probably won't for another five. I haven't even got his phone number on my mobile.

I did bump into both of them at our mate's wedding in December 2007. I was outside having a fag, and Richard came out and asked if I fancied playing a few songs. We did about four numbers, which was really weird. Later that night, Kelly and I talked long into the night. We necked down a bottle of Jack Daniel's and both agreed to stay in touch. We haven't talked since.

As far as Kelly is concerned, he will survive. He is still a super-talented guy, but I don't think he personally or the band itself is really progressing from where they were several years ago. And I don't think the public are really interested in what he's got to say any more. Maybe he'd be better off working with a great producer, someone like Brian Eno. Perhaps he just needs someone else to take control and produce the music for a chance. Maybe he should do a bit of a 'Paul Weller' and expand out to do some other kind of music, either solo or go and write songs with someone else for a while, just to take the pressure off. Then he might smile, as in the old days. I think he could get a record deal himself if anything ever happened to the band, even if it is just Kelly doing some type of classic cover songs, like that great one he did of 'Gladrags'. To be honest, I think something like that could give him his biggest success on both sides of the Atlantic.

As for me, as far as playing ever again with the Stereophonics is concerned, maybe one day we will get back together. I can see us in about thirty years' time when the money starts to dry up, playing in Minehead Butlin's on one of those tribute-band weekends, 'The Britpop Tribute Years'. We will be on stage, in the Beachcomber Bar, while Oasis will be in the Pig and Whistle,

Pulp in the Gaiety Ballroom and Supergrass playing out on the lawn before the Donkey Derby commences. What a mental weekend that would be!

Do I miss the old rock'n'roll lifestyle and living in the fast lane? Of course I do! I would be lying if I said I didn't. There are times when I would love to be strolling out to a packed house or making a new best-selling album. Would I have changed anything if I could rewind my life? Not much, really. Maybe I would have kept the bob haircut from the gig in the Aberdare Coliseum, and learning to play the drums might have been helpful. But, seriously, no: I did what I did in life and I can't look back. I just move on and turn over another page.

All in all, I don't think I've done that bad, considering. Let's take a peek at my life report so far:

- **played drums** in one of the biggest bands in the UK
- **sold millions** of albums and singles worldwide
- **travelled** all over the world, several times
- got a **beautiful boy**, Cian
- had my **own TV show**
- built up quite a **successful radio career**
- got a bit of **money** in the bank and **couple of houses** dotted about
- met some **wonderful people** over the years
- still meeting more and more **wonderful people** every day.

Not bad for a chopsey twat with curly hair from the best village in the world.

# LUCKY FOR STU?

'Stu's hair is only curly because he's too stubborn to grow it straight! As loud as the instrument he plays, witty like a snare drum, bolder than kick drum. He remembers *everything*, from song structure, quotes from films, TV shows, word-perfect – everything. Except the night before. His boy Cian is great, too. He bounces alongside Stuart like a balloon on a string, always full of energy, always inquisitive, with an endless back catalogue of questions to be answered. The apple doesn't fall far from the tree.'

**Greg Jones, singer, Killing for Company**

# CHAPTER 14

# KILLING FOR A LOOKALIKE

**W**ow, what a quick year it's been since I finished writing *Demons and Cocktails*. Doesn't time fly when you're having fun…or when you're just enjoying life? Anyway, I thought with the release of the paperback version of the book I would update you on what's been going on in the world of Cable.

First up, I must mention how great it was to add the word 'author' to my ever-expanding CV. I bet none of my teachers, or in fact most people who know me, ever thought they would hear the words *Stuart Cable* and *author* appear in the same sentence. But hey, for most of my life I have gone out of my way to prove people wrong!

*Demons and Cocktails* was released in May 2009 at a big glitzy launch party in Cardiff. It turned out to be a great night with many celebrities, family and friends turning up as well as reporters from TV, radio and the national press. Of course, in true rock star fashion, I don't remember much of the after party, but what do you expect when you end up drinking with Pritchard from *Dirty Sanchez* until the early hours of the morning?

The book itself propelled me back into the glare of the spotlight, with front-page headlines, interviews, TV appearances and book signings – although the book signing events were much less manic than the heady days of the record signings with the Phonics, which at times were mental to say the least! For our second album, we had a midnight signing in HMV in Cardiff and the crowds stretched right around the block several times. We didn't actually finish until 5am!

In contrast, the book events were more relaxed, with me meeting and greeting the surprisingly large number of people who took time out to not only buy the book, but more importantly to spend time chatting and discussing life. Of course lots of Stereophonics fans turned up for a copy, wanting to find out what went on behind the scenes, plus there were many fans of my radio and TV shows, and curiously a few drummers popped in. I've always said that being a drummer is like being in the Masons; we have our own code, our own language and of course we all worship the same Rock God, Mr Keith Moon. So it was great to meet these guys and talk about drum kits and gigs and other technical drumming stuff. The saying is true: 'Once a drummer, always a drummer'.

A real pleasant surprise was the number of people who knew very little about my past life with the band, but who turned up after reading excerpts from the book in the national press and who thought it was such a good read that they wanted more.

One of the main stories from the book, and the story that got me the publishing deal in the first place, was the one about me,

## KILLING FOR A LOOKALIKE

Keith Richards and the now famous shepherd's pie. It was amazing how the world's press picked up on the pie story and within 24 hours of it appearing in the *Wales on Sunday*, it spread like wildfire all around the globe. The amount of times it appeared on the internet and in newspapers around the world was unbelievable. It was even mentioned on *Loose Women*!

Obviously, before the book's release I was quite nervous and scared about how it would be received. I'd set out to write the book mainly about the wonderful times I'd had and to get some closure but I definitely didn't write it to take a vindictive swipe at Kelly or Richard. And the feedback was much better than I'd imagined it would be. I lost count of the number of people who told me how much they enjoyed it, and even though it was a rather candid and a full-on warts-and-all account of my life, everyone who read it commented how much it made them laugh out loud from start to finish. Most of them said that when they started reading it they couldn't put it down; lots of people apparently finished it in one or two sittings. The biggest compliment any author could receive.

Even Kelly's brother gave me a big thumbs-up when I met him in Cwmaman a few weeks after it came out. I'm not sure if the great man himself has bought a copy, but knowing Kelly, he has, and I really hope he liked what he read. It did come from the heart.

John Brand, the ex-Stereophonics manager who now manages Killing for Company, wants to turn the book into an audiobook, which I think would be good especially if we could break it up with songs and maybe some original interviews. We'll see. Also there has been talk about selling the film rights; maybe that's a bridge too far, but who knows in this crazy world? Some casting director could soon be searching for three lucky Welsh boys to play a curly-haired, big-nosed idiot who hits drums, a slightly small, good-looking moody genius, and a six-foot mute covered in tattoos!

On the subject of Kelly, we've talked a bit over the last year and we still text each other on occasions. He called me up out of the blue on Christmas to tell me he'd been listening to Tragically Hip records and it brought back great memories of our early days. I called him up to congratulate him when the Phonics played their successful return gig at Cardiff Castle, a full 11 years since our first bash there. Most of my mates had gone to see the show and when they got back to the Welsh Harp they were more than happy to rub it in and tell me how good it had been. I called Kelly up straight away that night to say well done and he asked me to come down to have a couple of beers – but I was already well oiled by then so I didn't go.

I'm more than positive we will meet up in the near future and I'm sure it will be an emotional time together. I'm really pleased for the band and Kelly, and glad that they are still one of the best live bands in the country and making great songs.

But enough of the past; time to move on. The biggest thing for me over the past year has been the progression of Killing for Company. Most of the early part of 2009 was really frustrating for the band, when attempts to get us into the recording studio stalled as contracts between us and the record label were drawn up, then ripped up, written again, ripped up again and changed, but finally, after what seemed like a lifetime, everything was agreed. The downside of all the uncertainty was that we'd hardly organised any gigs for that time because we thought we'd be recording. It was a disappointing time because we missed out on both the studio work and playing live. On the plus side, though, it did give us the opportunity to write some new material together and it gave us time to really get to know each other and to bond tightly as friends as well as band members both on and off stage.

In August 2009, with all the wrangling with the record company sorted out, we all headed off to sunny Newcastle to spend four weeks in the studio recording our first (of many) albums, entitled *Lost Art of Deception*. For me it was great to be back in that environment, making an album and being an active part of the creative process again, and of course being part of the 'get drunk because I'm a rock star' process!

It was a tight schedule as we aimed to do it all in just a month, with another 10 days pencilled in a few weeks later to mix it. Due to my radio commitments back in Wales, I often had to travel back home, but all in all it worked out well, and for my part I bashed out 14 songs in five days to lay down the foundation for the others. I love the feeling of the studio, but believe it or not it can be a lonely and sometimes stressful place in that booth with the rest of the band sitting outside watching and listening to your every beat. The pressure can be intense, and you don't want to let the team down, but when it's over it's time to enjoy it.

If I've come across as a bit of a creep by stating that making music is the hardest thing in the world, sorry, and I would like to apologise to all the hard-working people out there who make a living doing a 'proper' job. In fact making music is the opposite actually; it's a great life being a musician no matter what some down-on-their-luck, straight-out-of-rehab star writes in their memoirs. It's a privileged way to earn a living, especially when everything and everyone in the band is on fire.

Next up in the studio after my drumming, Steve, Andy and Richie added the guitars, which took another 10 days, which left Greg to add his magic with the vocals. Greg was still working full-time, so the rest of us wanted to make sure everything was done for him when he got to the studio. Again, he didn't disappoint, doing all his wonderful vocals in five days. Like I said, it was a tough schedule but we did it and it was great the way we all worked together to make the songs come to life. It was so different from the Stereophonics sessions, especially the last two albums I was involved in where Kelly called most of the shots. The Killing for Company sessions were much more relaxed, more of a team effort with all of us chipping in. We even worked up some new songs as we went along.

But it wasn't all work and no play. One night while in the middle of the final mix, Andy and I decided to pop across the road to have a quiet drink in a nightclub. As we approached, the bouncer recognised me and let us in for free, and then it got even better, or maybe worse, because the barman turned out to be a huge Phonics fan and instead of getting us two glasses of vodka, he simply gave us the entire bottle of Absolut with the compliments of the house.

It would have been rude to refuse, so what was supposed to be a few quiet beers turned into a full session with us staggering home at 6am '*Absolut*-ely' legless. I collapsed on the floor outside my room, until Steve, who I was sharing with, dragged me in and put me to bed.

When I woke up I had the hangover from hell, but I somehow

came round enough to head off to the studio to help with the mixing. On the way, we stopped at the shops for some supplies and for some reason – only the devil knows why – I bought a litre of my favourite drink, Jack Daniels. At the studio I proceeded to drink it all by myself. Apparently I was quite funny in the beginning, having a laugh and clowning about, but soon I crossed the line and became a right royal pain in the arse. I got howling drunk before passing out again. That was one of the worst drinking experiences I've ever had – I thought I was going to die! 'Stuart, don't go near the light,' I'm sure I heard Steve saying when he tried his best to wake me up…

But that's all part of the fun.

We finished the album and I'm really, really proud of what we've done. With John Brand on a mission to create another new sensation, who knows where it will take us!

After the album was finished, we started gigging again and one of the most enjoyable times we had was supporting The Alarm at the annual event called The Gathering. It's a weekend thing held at Prestatyn Holiday Camp each year where fans come from all over the world. We had a great craic and because of our performance the legend that is Mike Peters became a big fan and asked us if we would support The Alarm on a big tour across the UK in May 2010, which we have started as I write these pages. Who says a man can't multi-task?

It's funny how life revolves around in one big circle. It only seems like yesterday that Kelly, Richard and I were at the bottom of the gigging ladder, travelling around to shows in my little yellow van. Of course that all changed when everything exploded for us. Gigs and tours were a lot more enjoyable and normally meant top-class hotels, with us three just turning up to the gig, playing and partying afterwards. Now, as it all starts again for me, I can't believe that one of the jobs on my list is to sit at home booking hotels on the internet for the Alarm tour. I must say I didn't realise how many Travelodges there were in the UK, and how bloody long it takes to organise things like that!

Outside of the music scene, I still like to do a spot of 'socialising' and it still gives me the biggest kick of all to get out and meet people of all ages and just relax and be myself.

One of the funniest things to happen to me on one of my many 'socialising' nights was the time I went to a surprise retirement party in Llanelli Railway Club in West Wales with some close friends. For people who are not aware, Llanelli is a town famous for once having a wonderful rugby side, and – hopefully the town won't take this the wrong way – nothing much else.

As soon as I got there, I had a feeling the night was going to be interesting, to say the least. The first thing I noticed was the fact that all of the men and boys in the room were wearing near-identical checked shirts. The place itself was a cross between the club in Peter Kay's show *Phoenix Nights* mixed with elements of the film *The Hills Have Eyes*. On stage, there was this guy with thick plastic glasses singing away like a scalded cat. The guy turned out to be the steward of the club and during the night he popped up everywhere – on stage singing, playing guitar, behind the bar, calling the bingo, even making the sandwiches. I kept seeing him wherever I looked. At one stage I was convinced it wasn't the same bloke and maybe there were eight of the fuckers floating about!

As I went to the bar a boy came up to me and grunted, 'Hey,

fuckin' hell mate, you look like Stuart Cable!' I laughed and carried on, thinking he was having a laugh. Then, by the bar, a woman turned around and said more or less exactly the same thing, but with a few more 'fuckin's thrown in for good measure.

'Thank you,' I replied, deciding to play along with the gag. 'Lots of people tell me that.'

'Fuckin' hell,' she shrieked out, 'You fuckin' sound like him as well!' Everyone around her nodded in agreement.

'I *am* him,' I answered rather sheepishly.

'Fuck off. What would Stuart Cable be doing in Llanelli?'

I stood speechless and even when I pulled my wallet out to show her my credit card with my name on it, she still wouldn't believe me. 'You could get one of them anywhere,' she said, strolling away with her two pints of lager.

It got even better when I went back to my seat and the entertainment started. I know I'm from Cwmaman, which is not exactly the centre of the entertainment world, but I swear the artists on stage that night would have made the cast of *Deliverance* look like acts at the Royal Variety Performance. There were singers of all shapes and sizes, dancers with bits missing, and halfway through the night I'm sure the steward got back up on stage to perform his speciality – putting a ferret down his trousers.

However, I didn't have it all my own way when a comedian, who had flown over from Spain especially for the night, came on with a glint in his eye. He wore a bad toupée, his clothes looked like they came from 1974 and he was sweating like a rapist hiding in a bush. He proceeded to have a go at me because he reckoned I had a Jesus look going on. 'I bet you shit yourself when Easter comes around,' he mocked me.

Of course this brought the house down. To be fair it was rather funny at first – but after the sixtieth time hearing the same type of joke, it started to get on my tits.

Another funny thing happened before I left, when a couple of boys (with their checked shirts hanging over their jeans) came over to talk. One of them said, pointing to the boy next to him, 'Hey Stu…my mate bought a set of drums belonging to you on eBay.'

'Has he?' It made me wonder.

The boy proudly showed me a photo of the drum kit on his mobile phone; the grin stretching wide across his face.

I know I shouldn't have but I couldn't resist it. 'Sorry mate, but those are not mine,' I said honestly. 'I've never had a set like that.'

The smile fell off the boy's face as he sulked off with his mates taking the piss out of him for the rest of the night.

Maybe I'm being a bit unfair about the place; it turned out to be a good night and they were great to me after a slow start, and I can't wait to go back again!

By the time this edition of my book hits the shelves, I will have reached another milestone in my life…the BIG 4-0.

It's strange – when you're young and a little wet behind the ears you never imagine you will ever reach that age. And I don't mean that in an 'I hope I die before I get old' way, it just seemed like a different world altogether when you're growing up. But now I'm here, I don't feel any different. Maybe I've got a few more grey hairs, I'm a little fatter around the edges, and there are a couple more wrinkles around the eyes, but thankfully everything is still in working order.

So, as my secret 40th birthday bash is no doubt being organised,

## KILLING FOR A LOOKALIKE

I've been looking back to the year before and my secret 39th birthday party. Now that was another night to remember, or maybe to forget. First off, I nearly ruined the surprise my mates had set up for me in the Welsh Harp when I threw my toys out of the pram because I'd accidentally shaved half my goatee off when trying out my new electric beard razor. I didn't realise how powerful it was! I was gutted and phoned my mate to tell him I wasn't going out.

Apparently, while I pouted about in my house, my mates sat in the pub pissing themselves. Finally when I'd cooled down and shaved the rest of my beard off, I went out for a much-needed pint. Deep down I had a feeling something was going on but it was still a great surprise to walk in to the Welsh and see how many friends had turned up.

After a good session we ended up in my house and predictably, after everyone refused to shut up and listen to AC/DC with me at three in the morning, I got pissed off, finished the rest of the Jack Daniels and collapsed in the front room.

Everyone thought I was dead. Yet in typical Welsh fashion, instead of trying to make sure I was OK, Bunko and Ed, my so-called mates, decided that it would be a financially sound idea to sign as many things as they could with my name on just in case I did die, so that they could make some money selling the stuff on eBay. So with markers in hand they set about the house signing everything they could. Sadly for them I did survive to fight another day, and for weeks afterwards I was still finding items with my name on around the house. Onions, garlic, pots, pans, slippers, wooden spoons, mugs and even the cooker! That's what friends are for.

## DEMONS AND COCKTAILS

Reaching 40 is an important landmark in anyone's life. Hopefully for me it will not just be a case of a new chapter in my life, but the start of a new book altogether. Life's too short to live in the past; it's all about looking forward and enjoying it. Hopefully with my new adventure with Killing for Company and with my new radio show back on the BBC called *Saturday Night Cable*, I can finally put *Demons and Cocktails* away on the shelf for good. And the next time I write again will be when I reach the grand old age of 50 and then the book will be entitled:

> '*The Best Ten Years of my Life* – by the totally
> teetotal and super-fit Stuart Cable,
> the Duke of Cwmaman'

# AFTERWORD

**T**o be given the opportunity to combine my love for music with my passion for writing, while working with Mabel Cable's second son on this book, has been like a dream come true. Over the past six months or so, I've met some special people, been to some great places and drunk numerous pints of Guinness in the Welsh Harp, all in the name of research. But the most exciting part for me was being able to travel with Stuart back through his memories. At times it was a rough old, tough old ride, but as I got lost in his rock'n'roll world, I actually felt as if I were the one cutting Cian's umbilical cord, or signing the record deal with Kelly and Richard, and even eating the great Keith Richards' shepherd's pie by mistake, and all the rest of the remarkable stuff Stuart did.

I found him to be a really special guy, always willing to give people his time and attention. He is such a people person, it's incredible. I've enjoyed every minute of it, even the many drunken nights when we've ended up arguing (and once nearly fighting out on the grass at three in the morning) about who were the better band, the Clash or that out-of-tune pub band from Australia.

I can't thank him enough for sharing his life with me and I hope it's just the start of a long friendship. But before I go, I would just like to leave him with two last things: first, Joe Strummer is God, and last, no one from Snakes-ville has ever beaten someone from Merthyr in a fight. Ever. Fact.

Mr Cable,
Step lightly, Stay Free

Bunko
X

www.stuartcable.co.uk
www.anthonybunko.com
www.elliepr.com